Globalization
and Well-Being

 Brenda and David McLean
Canadian Studies Series

Other books in the series:

W.H. New, *Borderlands:*
How We Talk about Canada

Alan C. Cairns, *Citizens Plus:*
Aboriginal Peoples and the Canadian State

Cole Harris, *Making Native Space:*
Colonialism, Resistance, and Reserves in British Columbia

Globalization

and
WELL-BEING

JOHN F. HELLIWELL

UBCPress · Vancouver · Toronto

09 08 07 06 05 04 03   5 4 3 2

Printed in Canada on acid-free paper

National Library of Canada Cataloguing in Publication Data
Helliwell, John F., 1937-
   Globalization and well-being / John F. Helliwell.

   Includes bibliographical references and index.
      ISBN 0-7748-0992-2 (bound); ISBN 0-7748-0993-0 (pbk.)

   1. Globalization – Social aspects. 2. Quality of life. 3. Canada – Social
conditions – 1991- 4. Political planning – Canada. I. Title.

HF1359.H43 2002   337   C2002-911120-X

Canadä

This book has been published with the support of the K.D. Srivastava Fund.
UBC Press also gratefully acknowledges the financial support for our
publishing program of the Government of Canada through the Book
Publishing Industry Development Program (BPIDP), and of the Canada
Council for the Arts, and the British Columbia Arts Council.

Set in Aldus by Echelon Design
Text design: Echelon Design
Printed by Friesens
Copy editor: Joanne Richardson
Proofreader and indexer: Deborah Kerr

UBC Press
The University of British Columbia
2029 West Mall
Vancouver, BC V6T 1Z2
604-822-5959 / Fax: 604-822-6083
www.ubcpress.ca

Contents

Acknowledgments

HERE IS WHERE I SHOULD MAKE MY THANKS. THESE LECTURES BUILD ON more than thirty years of activity in diverse lines of research, supported by colleagues and friends near and far, inspired and aided by generations of students and research assistants, and financed by a host of institutions and granting councils. Any attempt to spell out these debts in detail would be subject to many failures of omission. What can be done, beyond this general admission of inadequate gratitude? First and most important, I can point to my largest debt, too seldom acknowledged in more detailed lists of thanks found in my academic works. But here, where specific lists are impossible, the general debt finds its place. It is, of course, to my wife Millie (or Judith, as she is known in her passport and by some of her legions of friends), who has been wise counsellor, loving helpmate, family glue, and inspiring friend for more than thirty years of life in ten cities spread over seven countries. Our sons David and James, big contributors in their own right, join me in admiring her ability to create new homes and communities wherever we have been while never losing touch with the rest of our supporting web. This book is mainly about the sources of well-being, and she has been our inspiration and guide in what lies behind the words and the numbers.

The only other debt of equal duration is that to the University of British Columbia, which has been my main base camp for almost half a century, ever since I entered as a freshman in 1954. I have known and loved the university as student, buildings and grounds worker, teaching assistant, and, for more than thirty-five years, as a faculty member in the department of economics. We have in many ways grown up together, and I welcome the chance to thank all those who still remain of the thousands of colleagues and friends who have built UBC. Most recently, by inviting me to fill the Brenda and David McLean Chair of Canadian Studies for two years they have given me the impetus and the opportunity to prepare these lectures, while the Christiansen Fellowship of St Catherine's College, Oxford, gave me the chance to develop the new research on well-being that marks the biggest change from the original lectures to the form that they take in this book.

Hornby Island
July 2002

Introduction

THIS BOOK HAS THREE CHAPTERS, BASED ON THREE BRENDA AND DAVID McLean Lectures given at Green College at the University of British Columbia in November 2000. Over the following months, these lectures have been extended and updated to reflect subsequent events and research, and to provide a larger gap, in both time and content, between this book and my C.D. Howe Benefactors Lecture (Helliwell 2000), which deals with many of the same issues. The McLean Lectures, and this book, deal with, and contrast, what is known and what is thought about several key aspects of Canada's past and future. The first chapter sets the stage by reviewing the latest evidence on the extent to which globalization has altered the scope and salience of nation-states; the second chapter deals with implications for domestic policies; and the third chapter deals with international policies. Relative to the original lectures, this book, as its title suggests, places increased emphasis on well-being as an explicit focus for research and for public policies.

A personal history of ideas may help to explain the structure and content of this book. I have always been an empirically based researcher, dedicated to using data to understand the past and present, and to reveal possibilities for the future. As I have delved into the issues of the day, I have several times in the past thirty years come across evidence that forced me to rethink my view of the world. Sometimes the facts came to light in the course of my own researches, as when, in the early 1970s, what seemed a routine study of the macroeconomic consequences of a proposal to build a natural gas pipeline down the Mackenzie Valley led to the discovery that the underlying microeconomics of the proposal were dramatically weaker than was believed by proponents, regulators, and governments. Several years of subsequent research confirmed that what was then seen as an energy supply crisis in Canada was really nothing of the sort. Policies driven by the perception of Canadian energy shortage led to needless private and taxpayer losses, while contributing to the decay of public trust in both business and government capacity to deliver equitable and efficient solutions. I and other researchers did what we could to limit these losses.

At other times the evidence forcing me to rethink my view of the world, and to redirect my own researches accordingly, came from reading research written by others. Thus in the early 1990s I first saw an unpublished working paper by John McCallum showing that trade intensities among Canadian provinces were an order of magnitude greater than were those between Canadian provinces and US states. This paper, later revised and published (McCallum 1995), was so much at odds with what I had previously assumed, and indeed written (Helliwell 1989), about globalization that it forced me to dramatically redirect my own research. His findings were either of fundamental importance to economic theory, and to the possibilities and need for national and international policies, or else they were somehow mistaken. So much was at stake that I had to try to discover which was the case. This led to collaborative work with McCallum (Helliwell and McCallum 1995) and to further research, by myself and many others. This research is the focus of the first of the McLean Lectures and lies at the heart of Chapter 1. The burden of this research is that McCallum's original result stands the tests of replication and still persists in Canada and in other countries, even if no other data can be quite as appropriate as those comparing interprovincial with province-state trade. One implication of this result, noted early on (Helliwell 1996b), is that the economic structure of Canada was much tighter than was assumed in debates about the economic consequences of Quebec independence.

A second and more general implication is that there is much more scope and need for national policies than one would think from widespread media and other commentaries about the irrelevance of the nation-state. As often happens, a second key fact came to light as a by-product. The McCallum and subsequent research makes use of the gravity model, which explains economic linkages by the size of economic units and the distance between them, just as in Newton's original formulation of the law of gravity. McCallum added a variable for the national border and showed that being in the same country generated a great deal more trade. By appropriately comparing the sizes of the estimated effects of distance and national borders, it is possible to compute the effect of the national border in terms of an equivalent distance – more than 10,000 miles in the case of McCallum's estimates of distance and border effects (Helliwell 2002a). This calculation is even more striking when one takes into account another dramatic feature of the gravity equations – that distance reduces the intensity of trade flows by far more than could be explained by transportation costs (Grossman 1997; Hazledine 2000). The likely reasons for this are assessed in Chapter 1, and they relate to the social and information networks that facilitate economic and social collaboration. One of the consequences of this is that economies are not just more national but also more local than is commonly assumed. This has implications for both national and international policies, as is discussed in Chapters 2 and 3.

Two more revelations are worth mentioning since they have a great influence on the structure and content of Chapters 2 and 3. Both relate to the importance of the social and institutional fabric of a society, and the need for policies to take these fully into account. The first revelation has been the stubborn failure of many of the countries of the former USSR to achieve the hoped-for economic and social progress that was expected to follow the fall of the Berlin Wall in 1989. It was always understood that there are important institutional requirements that must be met if an economy and society are to function well, but economists and others have tended to presume that where education levels were high enough the necessary institutions would eventually evolve. What was not adequately foreseen was that the post-1990 institutional gaps would be filled faster by the Mafia than by the rule of law and that levels of GDP per capita in large parts of the former USSR would fall by half over the subsequent decade, even as they were doubling in the much more closed economy of China. This experience has forced researchers and policy makers alike to conduct their institutional analysis more seriously.

The second revelation adds to the importance of the first by showing that many of the same features of society that are needed to support a successful economic transition are of even greater importance to broader measures of well-being. This has no doubt been long understood by others, but it became obvious to me only when I started to systematically study the determinants of life satisfaction in many countries over the past twenty years. It turns out, as will be explained in more detail in Chapter 2, that measures of trust and social capital, which have been previously studied mainly in relation to their impacts on economic growth and human mortality, have strong effects on well-being in addition to those effects operating indirectly through incomes and health. Furthermore, these direct effects are becoming relatively more important as time passes since they are not subject to the diminishing returns that appear to mark the effects of increases in both absolute and relative incomes. These findings, many of which are still tentative, have forced me to take an ever-broader and more interdisciplinary approach to the study of local, national, and global society. I cannot promise to have made these extensions in such a way as to satisfy all of the disciplines involved, but the stakes are high enough, in my view, to justify the effort and to support the risks. The results thus far are reported in Chapters 2 and 3.

1 Globalization and the Nation-State

WHAT IS MEANT BY GLOBALIZATION? LET ME START WITH THREE OR four views held by those standing on different parts of the world stage. For protestors in Seattle, Gothenberg, or Genoa, globalization represents a state of the world wherein international organizations implement the wishes of transnational corporations, ensuring that free trade rules will combine with global market pressures to eliminate the ability of local and national governments to implement policies. In this view Coca-Colonization already prevails and only the details remain to be settled. The protestors include an uneasy combination of anarchists who, for a variety of reasons, wish the worst for all governments, whether political or commercial, and reformers who see a need for an expanded international agenda that places more weight on debt relief, the environment, labour standards, or some other set of issues thought to be stalled or lost in the open trade agenda.

Within corporations and business groups, globalization usually refers to a global market reach and to an imperative that firms must "globalize or die." In this view, firms that do not take the world as their market will simply find themselves outflanked and out-gunned. Firms with a national base aim for international markets, suppliers, and partners, and argue for domestic tax rates that are at least as low as are those in competing jurisdictions.

Most national governments are ambivalent about the meaning

and consequences of globalization. Views also differ according to political regime and the current state of development. Smaller countries, especially the richer among them, have tended to think internationally for much longer than have the larger countries, if only because world markets have been more essential to their success. Countries that are the main sources of international direct investment, and the main bases for international manufacturing capacity, generally favour more open trading arrangements; but here too there is a crucial difference between large and small. A rules-based system, with international arbitration and enforcement, is highly valued by the smaller countries as their best defence against the use of power to settle trade disputes. For the larger countries, and especially for the United States, the ceding of rule making and enforcement to international jurisdiction is seen as a dangerous encroachment of national sovereignty. In poorer countries, and especially the smaller among them, there is also ambivalence about the nature and consequences of globalization. Most recognize that finding solutions to their own problems will require access to global sources of knowledge, market opportunities, and perhaps capital. However, many citizens of poorer countries fear that global markets will lead to exploitation of their natural and human resources for immediate foreign advantage with little residual benefit for themselves and their children. There is a parallel concern, expressed widely at the Seattle meetings of the World Trade Organization (WTO), that the rich countries are intent upon opening developing country markets for rich-country exports while refusing to allow poor countries to have free access to rich-country markets for poor-country exports (i.e., indigenously produced food and textiles).

Among economists, globalization refers to a situation where the so-called "law of one price" applies on a global basis. This assumes that goods and services will be freely and costlessly traded over space and borders. This has been the standard model in the theory of international trade for decades, with only tariffs and sometimes transport costs creating wedges between prices in different countries. The standard trade models have, however, tended to treat labour and (often) business capital stock as fixed factors and, hence, as not mobile across national borders. Sometimes globalization is taken to describe a process wherein markets are becoming more global as time passes. Through the use of a number of measures economic historians have documented that markets for many goods and services have been becoming more global over the past half-century, largely reversing de-globalizing changes over the first half of the twentieth century.

Many of those who were aware of the great increases in international trade in the second half of the twentieth century were less aware of the scale of the reductions during its first half. In any event, at least until the publication of McCallum's results and those of an independent parallel study by Engel and Rogers (1996), economists, like those less involved with economic affairs, assumed that, in the absence of tariffs or other border impediments, trade in goods and services would be just as intense among countries as within them, especially if due account were taken of the effects of distance. Thus it was widely thought that by the 1990s national and international trade were taking place at roughly similar intensities.

When first engaged in research designed to test and extend the McCallum results, I made several informal surveys to see if I was the only one who was surprised. In several groups, containing varying proportions of trained economists, I asked whether 1988 Canadian merchandise trade intensities were greater north-south or east-west. More precisely, I asked audiences to estimate the ratio of province-province trade intensities against those between provinces and states. They were to give the answer 1.0 if they thought the two intensities were equal; 0.5 if north-south trade flows were twice as intense as east-west flows; and 2.0 if, after allowing for the effects of economic size and distance, interprovincial trade intensities were twice as great as those between provinces and states. The term "border effect" is often used to describe the extent to which national boundaries influence trade patterns. If those surveyed thought that there was no border effect, then they would answer 1.0; a figure of less than 1.0 would mean that north-south trade was more intense than interprovincial trade; and a value greater than 1.0 would signal greater national trade densities. In a sample of about 100 graduates in economics, political science, and psychology, the average answer given was 0.8, with most respondents thinking that, if anything, trade intensities were greater north-south than east-west (Helliwell 1996b).

Thus I was not the only one to be surprised by McCallum's finding that 1988 interprovincial merchandise trade flows were more than twenty times more intense than were those between provinces and states. For example, Ontario is about the same distance from California as it is from British Columbia, and the Californian population and GDP are about ten times larger than are those of British Columbia. Thus one would expect to find, if there were no systematic differences between interprovincial and province-state trade, that two-way movements of goods between Ontario and California were ten times larger than were those between Ontario and British Columbia. But actual merchandise flows between British Columbia and Ontario were more than twice as large as were those between California and Ontario, or twenty times greater than expected. Of course, McCallum's results related to 1988, the year before the Canada-United States Free Trade Agreement (FTA) was signed. In the aftermath of that agreement there have been large increases in north-south merchandise trade flows. These were sufficient to reduce the border effect from seventeen in 1981 to about twelve in 1996 (Helliwell 1998, 22). Indeed, these increases have been so large, and the associated productivity gains so small, as to raise puzzles in their own right. Economic models of the expected future consequences of the FTA projected that Canadian exports to the United States would increase by one-third and that imports would rise by 12 percent, in both cases holding income unchanged. The associated gains in Canadian productivity were projected to be equivalent to 8 percent of GDP per capita. But the actual trade increases, even after adjusting for the effects of rising incomes in the two countries, were more than three times as large as had been projected (Helliwell, Lee, and Messinger 1999), while GDP per capita grew more slowly in Canada than in the United States, with no evidence of a narrowing of the productivity gap. To some extent the pattern of productivity changes is what would be expected, with those industries facing the largest increases in international competition and market opportunities also having larger productivity gains (Trefler 1999). However, there is still the puzzle of why the increases in trade were larger than expected (based on the size of the tariff reductions) but that there was little or no sign of any narrowing of the long-standing manufacturing productivity gap between the two countries. I'll return to this puzzle later. First, however, I offer a summary of more recent evidence on the extent and consequences of globalization.

The McCallum result suggests strongly that national economies have a much tighter internal structure than was previously thought and, hence, that the extent of globalization is much less than is commonly supposed. First it was necessary to see if this result applies more generally in other places, other times, and other markets. Then it was necessary to explain why this could be the case, and why perceptions were so far from reality. If the result was found to be explicable, and of general application, then it would be time to assess its implications for private decisions and for public policies. This seems a simple enough research strategy, but it turns out to be not so easy to follow, for reasons that may also help to explain why perceptions were so far from the evidence uncovered by McCallum. It was not an accident that McCallum's research related to 1988 and only to 1988. Statistics Canada had developed full estimates of bilateral merchandise trade for the years 1984 through 1988 based on surveys of manufacturers and prepared as part of a consistent estimation of provincial and national accounts. There are still no other countries that have such fully developed measures of internal trade. Second, in anticipation of post-FTA interest in a detailed monitoring of the trade flows between Canada and the United States, from 1988 on

Statistics Canada started publishing bilateral merchandise imports and exports between Canadian provinces and US states.

McCallum realized that these two data sources could be combined so as to provide, for the first time, a direct comparison of the domestic and international trade intensities. He also realized the necessity of making the comparisons in a way that permitted trade intensity to be measured separately from the effects of size and distance. By choosing comparison pairs of equal distance, as when trade between Ontario and California is compared to that between Ontario and British Columbia, it is possible to make allowance for distance. But the gravity model is a better bet as it permits all trading pairs to be used together to give a single average size for the border effect. So the gravity model is what he used to produce his startling result, and he backed it up with enough specific examples to convince readers that the statistical result was not flowing from some extreme and unrepresentative observations.

One of the general difficulties in separating the effects of distance from those of borders is that, almost by definition, the borders of a country contain cities or provincial economies that are closer to each other than they are to cities or provinces in some other country. However, the unusual economic and political geography of Canada and the United States, with most of the Canadian population perched along the northern US border and the border itself swooping south into the US heartland, ensures that the average bilateral distance between Canadian provinces is very close to the average distance between the Canadian provinces and the thirty major trading states used in McCallum's analysis. Furthermore, each Canadian province has both provincial and state trading partners that are near and far, so there is no correlation between the border variable (used to denote province-state trading pairs) and the distance variable. Thus it was possible for McCallum to obtain strong and easily distinguishable effects of both distance and the national border. Much attention has been paid to the size of the border effects he discovered. Also important, and more easily replicated in other studies of international trade, is the large size of the distance effects. National borders greatly reduce trade intensities but so does distance, and to a far greater extent than can be explained by transport costs. I shall argue later that these two results can and should be explained in similar ways.

The unique nature of the Canadian data exposes a fundamental difficulty in replicating McCallum's research for other countries, other types of economic linkage, and earlier decades. It also helps to explain why everyone is surprised by McCallum's result. Even if earlier researchers had been interested in comparing intranational and international economic linkages, they had no data that would easily yield straightforward results. In the absence of data, researchers and commentators were inclined to assume, given all the talk of globalization and the widespread reporting of the large and growing volumes of international trade, that domestic and international economic linkages were comparably close.

Once I knew that my previous assumption was wrong, a multi-pronged research strategy was indicated: to prod the province-state merchandise trade results to see how they were concentrated by product and by region; to make comparable estimates for services; to trace the evolution of border effects in the wake of the FTA; to establish some methods for making comparable estimates for other countries; and finally to see to what extent there were comparable border effects for the movements of capital and population. At the same time, a full review of the international trade and linkage literature might help to reveal earlier studies that contained either direct or implicit evidence of border effects.

One very comparable study is that by Engel and Rogers, who were examining the co-variability of prices across city pairs, using a large number of Canadian and US cities. In the resulting paper "How Wide Is the Border?" (Engel and Rogers 1996), they showed that prices changed more in concert if cities were closer together or in the same country. This is, of course, just what one would expect after seeing the McCallum result since one of the classic motivations for trade is to arbitrage price gaps arising between markets in different locations. Buy bananas where they are cheap and sell them where they are expensive. If there is a greater volume of trading of this type, then one would expect to find prices moving in a more concerted way in the two markets. Since trade between provinces is much more dense than is trade between provinces and states, one would expect that prices are more closely aligned for city pairs that are in the same country. And this is what they found, reporting that the Canada-US border lowered price co-variability by as much as 2,500 miles of within-country distance. This estimate was based on their more conservative estimate of the effect of the border.

Subsequent research has shown that the effect of the border on price co-variability is far higher than they estimated. One obvious thing to check is whether the effect of distance on trade flows is the same for cross-border as for internal linkages. I did this for province-state and interprovincial trade flows, and found that the distance effect was the same in the two cases. However, when I re-estimated the Engel and Rogers equation, I found that the distance effect was significant for internal city pairs but that there was no effect for cross-border pairs. Since the width of the border is calculated from the relative sizes of the border and distance effects, this means that the implied width of the border is infinite. Furthermore, I discovered (Helliwell 2002a) that, even using their estimated distance effect as though it applied equally to cross-border pairs, the method of computation was not appropriate. Using the correct method raises the estimated width of the border to distances that have been described in parallel studies (Parsley and Wei 2000) as intergalactic.

Using the correct method to compute the distance equivalent of the border effect, the width of the Canada-US border is about 10,000 miles when estimated using merchandise trade flows, but it is many millions of miles, or even infinity, based on the co-variability of prices among city pairs (Helliwell 2002a). Thus the Engel and Rogers study strongly confirms the trade-based results. Indeed, their result appears even more extreme when the two results are expressed in somewhat comparable terms. What explains the sharp difference between these results? There are three reasons why there is so little cross-border price arbitrage in the data used by Engel and Rogers. The first and most important is that, in the short term, most consumer prices are rather stable, while foreign exchange rates are not. Thus by far the greatest source of cross-border discrepancy in two-monthly price changes (which are those studied by Engel and Rogers) is from changes in the exchange rate. The second reason is that their two-monthly price changes are probably too short term to trigger much in the way of transborder shipments. Finally, Engel and Rogers are using components of the consumer price index for their comparison, including both goods and services, and including in both cases the retail margins. By contrast, the trade results are based only on goods and exclude local retail margins. Other research has shown that services have substantially higher border effects, some two or three times greater than does merchandise trade (Helliwell 1998, 38), and local retail margins are less tradeable than are most other services. Together these three reasons provide powerful grounds for explaining the almost complete lack of cross-border price arbitrage of short-term changes in consumer prices. Most of this variability comes from the exchange rate and would in any event be arbitraged, if at all, by some cheaper means than changing cities for monthly haircuts or buying bananas in Toronto for consumption in Seattle.

To put the Engel and Rogers study into a broader context, there have been scores of studies of whether and when prices and exchange rates move so as to maintain purchasing power parity. As already noted, standard economic models of trade have long assumed that purchasing power parity would hold for so-called "tradeable goods," reflecting the "law of one price." In this setup, any international differences in prices were to be explained by differences in the prices of "non-tradeables," with labour-intensive services being the typical examples. Studies of purchasing power parity, especially those conducted since the general move towards flexible exchange rates in the early 1970s, showed that the world was at odds with the standard assumption. Three results proved general. First, foreign exchange rates are subject to short-term changes that are not immediately reflected in the prices of goods and services on either side of the border. Thus, just as was found by Engel and Rogers, short-term changes in nominal exchange rates lead to equivalent departures from purchasing power parity. Put slightly differently, changes in nominal exchange rates are generally matched, in the short-term, by equivalent changes in real exchange rates.[1] Second, if there is a move in prices or exchange rates towards purchasing power parity, it happens slowly, with the adjustment spread out over a period better measured in years than in months. Third, departures from purchasing power parity are as much in evidence for goods as for services, thus removing the possibility of explaining the lack of purchasing power parity as being simply due to the presence of non-tradeable goods and services. These results have been accumulating for many years. The Engel and Rogers study was the first to contrast them with domestic price movements, thus showing the extent to which international market linkages were less tight than were domestic ones.

There is another branch of the empirical trade literature that can be more easily understood in the light of strong border effects for trade. Tests of the standard theoretical model for international trade, the so-called Heckscher-Ohlin model, have consistently failed to find international trade patterns that reflect comparative advantage. However, more recent tests of the predictions of the model using regional trade flows within Japan find that Japanese regions do indeed specialize in those industries where the theory suggests they have a comparative advantage (Davis et al. 1997). This was thought to pose a puzzle: why should international trade models that have failed to predict the patterns of international trade nonetheless succeed at explaining the pattern of specialization of production within an economy? The reason, as suggested by the size and pervasiveness of border effects, is that the mobility assumptions underlying the classical trade theory do apply reasonably well within the Japanese economy but are a long way from being met for trade between countries. Perhaps the only thing wrong with traditional international trade theory is the word "international." It does work to explain domestic trade but fails to explain international trade because it neglects the variety of factors that separate markets, especially national markets: costly information, diverging knowledge and tastes, and transactions costs that grow substantially with distance and when one attempts to operate in a society with different norms and institutions.

Are there border effects also in capital markets? The answer is complicated, and the evidence often seems to say one thing while really indicating something else. The economic literature has tended to accept the assumption that there is a single world capital market for interest-bearing securities of equivalent risk so that international differences in interest rates would represent either a risk premium or an expected future change in the exchange rate. This fairly tight form of capital market integration is known as "uncovered interest parity" to distinguish it from "covered interest parity." Covered interest parity reflects a situation where international differences in nominal interest rates are exactly offset by a forward foreign exchange premium or discount. It is possible to test whether or not covered interest parity holds since it is often possible to obtain market prices for interest-bearing securities and for matching forward exchange contracts that permit an exact offset to the foreign exchange risk. Research has long shown that while the covered interest parity condition is not met exactly, it does tend to hold, except in times of market turbulence, within bounds that could reasonably be ascribed to transactions costs. The uncovered interest parity condition cannot be tested directly since it states only that the interest differential is equal to the expected change in the foreign exchange rate plus some allowance for the costs of carrying foreign exchange risk. Since neither the expected future exchange rate nor the risk premium can be directly measured, the theory itself is not directly verifiable.

Because of evidence supporting the covered interest parity condition, it has long been common for economists to assume that both the covered and the uncovered interest rate parity conditions hold. This implies that capital markets are perfectly linked internationally, that the forward exchange differential represents the expected rate of change in the exchange rate.[2] Any difference between the forward exchange differential and the actual future price of foreign exchange would thus represent some measure of foreign exchange risk plus, of course, random influences arising between now and then. The empirical fly in this theoretical ointment is that the forward exchange differential is typically a very bad predictor of the actual future change in the exchange rate. Indeed, the forward exchange rate is such a bad predictor of the future spot rate that it is beaten in the betting sweepstakes by the current value of the exchange rate. Thus the assumption that next year's exchange rate will be the same as today's is more accurate than is the forward exchange rate. In my view this long-standing result makes it a mistake to assume that the uncovered interest parity condition holds. I have tended to argue that the forward exchange rate differential is actually determined by the difference between the two national interest rates, so that the covered interest parity condition tends to hold fairly closely. But the fact that the forward exchange rate differential is such a bad predictor of future changes in the spot rate shows that the uncovered interest parity condition is a dangerous assumption. After all, if international capital markets were perfectly linked, then there would be many speculators willing to bet against the forward rate when it was a long way off base, thus making it a better predictor of the future spot rate. But there was no easy test of that presumption either, and the bulk of the exchange rate literature continued to treat international capital markets as completely integrated, at least for short-term financial capital.

In the light of a general assumption of tightly linked international capital markets, there was considerable scepticism when Feldstein and Horioka (1980) claimed that capital markets were still national rather than international in scope. They based their conclusion on a study of cross-country correlations between national savings rates and domestic investment rates. They reasoned that, if there were a single global capital market, then savings arising randomly in one country would be equally likely to be invested in any country and that investment booms in one country would be met from the global savings pool. So there would be no reason why countries with high savings rates would also have high investment rates. Sceptical theorists were quick to point out that domestic investment booms might lead to increases in national incomes and, through that route, to simultaneous increases in national savings even if international capital markets were perfectly linked. I was inclined to that view myself since I was operating an empirical open-economy macro model with just these features: investment booms would lead to increases in income and national savings even if the model were operated under the assumption of uncovered interest parity and, hence, of perfect international linkage of capital markets.

Fortunately, the same Statistics Canada efforts that gave rise to interprovincial trade data also provide provincial accounts that permit savings and investment to be defined on a provincial basis just as they are in the national accounts for Organization for Economic Co-operation and Development (OECD) countries. Thus it was possible to combine data from Canadian provinces and from OECD countries together into a single sample to obtain a more definitive test of the Feldstein and Horioka proposition. If Feldstein and Horioka were right to conclude that their results reflected international separation of national capital markets, then the correlation they found between national savings and domestic investment using country data would be markedly less for the Canadian provincial data. On the other hand, if the correlation were unrelated to national border effects, and if there were a single global capital market, then the correlation between savings and investment rates would be equally likely to arise among provinces as among countries. The research provided strong support for the Feldstein and Horioka interpretation. In the pooled sample there remains a strong correlation of savings and investment rates across countries but none across Canadian provinces (Helliwell and McKitrick 1999). Other studies using the less complete savings and investment data for regions within other countries show the same pattern.[3] Many repetitions of the Feldstein and Horioka tests, which tend to show some reductions in correlations as capital markets have become more integrated over the past twenty years, have combined with the evidence showing no correlations within national economies to convince a growing number of economists that the Feldstein and Horioka interpretation of their results is correct and that capital markets remain largely national in scope. This conclusion has been supported by studies of portfolio structure showing that investors routinely prefer to hold home-country rather than foreign equities (French and Poterba 1991; Baxter and Jermann 1997) and other studies showing no evidence that consumers borrow or lend abroad to smooth their consumption in the face of temporary fluctuations in income (Backus, Kehoe, and Kydland 1992).

Thus far we have confirmed that border effects for trade remain large for Canada and are matched by price linkages that are much tighter between national than international city pairs. Border effects for services are even larger than those for merchandise trade and show less evidence of having fallen in the wake of the FTA (Helliwell 1998, 38). Canadian and international evidence also indicates that capital markets are primarily national in scope. What can be done to get international evidence of border effects for merchandise trade? The key problem, as has been noted already, is that other countries do not have internal trade data as complete and comparable as are those among Canadian provinces. There have been two alternative approaches adopted in the face of this difficulty. One direct approach has been to use less complete internal trade data and to adopt different means of making them comparable to international trade statistics. This has, for example, been done by Gaudry, Blum, and MacCallum (1996) and Nitsch (2001) for German länder, and by Wolf (2000), Hillberry (1998, 1999), and Anderson and van Wincoop (2001) for US states. The results depend a great deal on the assumptions made to establish comparability of the internal and external trade data, with the result that Hillberry obtains much higher estimates of border effects for the United States than do Anderson and van Wincoop. The latter argue that the existence of many alternative domestic sources means that large countries like the United States might be expected to have much smaller border effects than are found for economies containing a smaller fraction of world GDP.

The other way of proceeding, initiated by Wei (1996) for the OECD countries, and since applied for them by Helliwell (1997, 1998 Chap. 3), Nitsch (2000a, 2000b), and Chen (2001); by Helliwell (1998, 57) for larger global samples of countries; and by Helliwell and Verdier (2001) to compare Canadian intra- and interprovincial trade, is to make use of input-output data to establish total final sales of merchandise, then subtracting exports to obtain a residual estimate of goods sold domestically. This provides a reasonable estimate of goods sold within the country, but application of the gravity model also requires an estimate of potential trading distances. The original method employed by Wei (1996) and Helliwell (1997, 1998) used one-quarter the distance from a country to its international trading partner. As noted by Nitsch (2000a), this method relies too much on the geography of the neighbouring countries and too little on the geography of the home country. Later studies have tended to use internal distance estimates that combine the theoretical structure of the gravity model with information about the distribution of population and economic activity within the country (Helliwell and Verdier 2001; Nitsch 2000b; Chen 2001; Helliwell 2002a). These more accurate estimates of internal distance are on average greater than those assumed by Wei and thus give larger estimates of border effects. On the other hand, more recent estimates of border effects also generally improve on the basic bilateral gravity model by including measures of each country's alternatives to trading with each of its bilateral trading partners, and this extension often results in lower estimates of border effects. All of the studies have shown significant border effects for the industrial countries and very much higher effects for developing countries. These effects are still large and significant even for trade between pairs of countries that have long been members of the European Union (EU). For example, even in the 1990s trade within typical EU members not sharing a common language was six times as intense as was international trade between them (Nitsch 2000b; Helliwell 1998, 51). Merchandise trade densities within developing countries were up to fifty or 100 times greater than was trade across national borders. Subsequent research suggests that some of these large differences in national border effects may be due as much to differences in the size of the economy as to differences in average per capita incomes (Anderson and van Wincoop 2001, Helliwell 2002c). Studies of trade flows by industry show that border effects tend to pervade all industries (Chen 2001; Helliwell 1998, 31). Finally, studies have shown that the inter-industry pattern of border effects is not explained by differences in the extent of non-tariff barriers (Head and Mayer 2000), so that any general explanation of border effects cannot just be based on the extent of remaining official barriers to trade.

Within Canada, much attention has been paid to the existence and possible effects of barriers to interprovincial trade. Recently improved measures of intraprovincial trade distances have permitted more useful estimates of the relative size of interprovincial and international border effects, which had previously been found to be insignificant for all provinces (Helliwell 1996b, 23-6). These new data show that, for the four largest provinces, there is no evidence that interprovincial trade is less dense than is intraprovincial trade, and for no province are the interprovincial border effects more than a fraction as large as are the international ones (Helliwell and Verdier 2001). Thus even the provincial differences of language, networks, and regulations have very little importance compared to those across national borders.

What are the likely causes of the separation of national markets? Until we have at least some preliminary answer to this question, we cannot make any judgments about whether this pooling of markets by nation is a good thing or a bad thing, and what if any may be the implications for public policies. Because studies have found that policy barriers are not an important cause of the remaining border effects among the industrial countries, the reasons must lie elsewhere. I have long been convinced that the underlying explanation must be able to deal simultaneously with border effects and the very large market-separating effects of distance. What happens to trade as distance grows, as borders are crossed, and as one moves from the known into the unknown (or at least the less familiar)? Being further from home usually means being less well connected to local networks, less able to understand local norms, and less able to be sure how much to trust what people may say. These changes occur as one gets further from familiar territory and are especially likely as one crosses national boundaries. This is because many institutions and legal systems are national in scope and differ much from one country to another.[4] Also, as will be reported later on, migration is much more likely within than across national borders, and migration and travel are primary means for extending knowledge and networks.

In order for the loss of network density and shared norms to be a primary cause of the very large border effects that have been discovered, one, or both, of two conditions must hold. Either the costs of trading over less dense networks are high, or the gains from additional long-distance international trade are modest. Or both. Let's look first at the importance of shared norms and networks, and the extent to which they are likely to decline with distance and as one crosses national borders. Consider an extreme case of what happens to trade and economic activity in the absence of a shared framework of rules and institutions. After the fall of the Berlin Wall in 1989, most students of economic development thought that the high levels of education and the generally widespread desire for democracy and open markets would lead to rapidly expanding trade and to a convergence of living standards between the parts of Europe that had been divided by the Iron Curtain. Yet in the decade after the fall of the wall, the largest parts of the former USSR, including Russia, Ukraine, and many of the smaller republics, saw not convergence towards western European living standards but, rather, a halving of their real GDP per capita.[5] At the time, the importance of reliable institutions, widely accepted norms, and high levels of mutual trust were seen to be important (Marer and Zecchini 1991), but no one foresaw the extent and costliness of their absence, or suspected how rapidly and successfully the Mafia would supplant legitimate business, and government corruption become rife, within an institutional vacuum.

The USSR experience provides an admittedly extreme example but is nonetheless useful. Smaller-scale studies of the cost-reducing effects of shared norms and networks, and of the effects of national boundaries and distance, are available. For example, studies of the spillover effects of R&D, which have been shown to depend considerably upon the strength and structure of networks of association and trust, have also been shown to decline strongly with distance (Keller 2002; Coe and Helpman 1995) and national borders (Helliwell 1998, 105). Similarly, international networks of high-tech workers migrating from India to Silicon Valley have been able to establish, through a process of "reputational intermediation" (Kapur 2001), long-distance business relations that would have been implausible in the absence of the mutual trust embodied in these personal networks. Similarly, the importance of mutual trust as a less costly and more effective replacement for complicated contracts and legal enforcement has long been recognized. The cost-reducing importance of informal networks and repeated contacts in building trust and validating informal contact has been emphasized in studies as diverse as explanations of the existence of the modern corporation (Hart 1995), the success of the northern Italian industrial districts, and the development of historical trade patterns and routes (Greif 1992).

If networks and trust are important in facilitating trade, and if the strength of these networks diminishes with distance and as borders are crossed, then this would be sufficient to explain why both distance and national borders mark steep reductions in the intensity of trade linkages. This explanation is probably increasingly accepted. If so, what does it imply? Should individuals and governments concentrate their efforts on increasing the density of international networks, working towards homogeneous institutions and cultures, in the hope that trade will thereby increase, with resulting improvements in national and global living standards? In the next chapter I shall discuss how living standards and other aspects of society interact in the determination of well-being. In this chapter I shall deal with the more limited issue of what economic benefits are likely to flow from expansions of international trade densities beyond those already existing among the industrial countries.

What is the evidence with regard to the effects of expanded trade upon growth and real incomes? One well-known study by Sachs and Warner (1995) divided developing countries into a closed and an open group, and found that the latter had shown significant convergence towards the higher living standards of the industrial countries while, on average, the former had shown no sign of closing the gap in living standards. In addition, Frankel and Rose (2000) have recently argued that countries that engage in more trade have significantly higher levels of GDP per capita than do countries that engage in less trade. My own interpretation of the Sachs and Warner evidence is that some degree of openness is likely to be required to permit the residents of a country to learn valuable lessons from abroad and to make the most of their own resources and talents. However, as the comparison of China and the former USSR in the 1990s starkly illustrates, openness is neither necessary nor sufficient to produce either growth or stability. Greater openness in the absence of robust domestic institutions may well hurt more than it helps. Since I have noted that border effects tend to be smaller for richer than for poorer countries (Helliwell 1998), my results are consistent with the Frankel and Rose finding that richer countries are more open to trade than are poorer countries. But how does the causality run?

To decide whether the richer industrial countries would be richer still if they were to change their policies so as to encourage international over domestic trade, it is perhaps most helpful to see whether the larger industrial countries are significantly richer than are the smaller ones. Why is this a useful exercise? Because the importance of national border effects means that larger countries already have larger and denser trading networks than do countries with smaller levels of aggregate GDP. The evidence shows no tendency for the large OECD countries to have per capita incomes higher than those of the smaller countries. This suggests that, for these countries, the major gains from comparative advantage trade have already been reaped and that further expansions of trade are likely to be based on increasing product variety, as represented by the number of brands on the shelves.[6] Indeed, many of the modern theories of international trade build on the fact that much of recent trade growth is of intra-industry rather than inter-industry exports and, thus, focus on product variety. The assumption that consumer welfare increases continually with the range of products available lies at the core of some recent large estimates of welfare gains from expanding trade (e.g., Anderson and van Wincoop 2001). However, psychological studies show that increasing the range of product choice becomes costly to buyers at a fairly early stage: they find it harder to make decisions when faced with many alternatives, take longer to reach their decisions, and are more likely to later regret their decisions (Iyengar and Lepper 1999). Thus it seems plausible, in the absence of demonstrated welfare benefits from trade densities beyond those already available among the industrial countries, to infer that the extra density of national over international networks may reflect a desirable state of affairs. If local networks have their own value, and are not foreclosing highly advantageous trading opportunities, then the fact that the resulting least-cost trading patterns have a high local and national content may well be just what the doctor ordered.

Exploring the Density of National Networks

The core of my favourite explanation for border effects is that it is cheaper and easier to operate within networks of shared norms and trust, and that the density of such networks declines with distance, especially as one crosses national borders. What evidence is there that networks and shared norms have important local and national features? There are two main dimensions that may be worth exploring. The first is based on the movements of people (because personal contacts are all-important in the establishment and maintenance of networks and trust). The second relates to the formal institutions that supplement, and sometimes substitute for, more informal personal networks. These include laws and the administration of justice, the design and implementation of standards, and the efficiency and quality of essential services, including (especially) health and education but also including the classic utilities – water, heat, light, power, and communications. If unfamiliar institutions and lack of trusted connections underlie the decay of trading and other densities with distance and across borders, then we would expect to find evidence of weaker personal contacts and more variety of institutional structure and quality where communities are separated by distance and borders.

There are two strands of the migration literature that help to shed light on the effects of distance and borders on the density of networks. The first relates to the extent that migration is altered by distance and by national borders. Using data from Canadian and US censuses, it is possible to model how both distance and national borders influence the probability of migration. The results are striking. The effects of distance are large, just as was seen to be true for trade flows. There are only half as many migrants from a province twice as far away. The effects of national borders are even greater for migration than for trade in goods and services. For example, there are only one-hundredth as many Canadian residents who were born in a US state as were born in another Canadian province, after taking due account of differences in size and distance (Helliwell 1998, 85-6). This border effect of 100 applies to residents of Canada. The bilateral national border effect is much smaller for those resident in the United States, reflecting the fact that over the past 100 years there have been three times as many Canadian-born moving to the US as US-born moving to Canada. It is noteworthy that these bilateral border effects have been increasing rather than decreasing as the fraction of the residents of one country who were born in the other has been on a fairly steady downward trajectory over the past 100 years. For example, in 1910 the number of Canadian-born individuals living in the United States was 20 percent as large as was the remaining population of Canada, while by 1990 this fraction had dropped to about 3 percent (Helliwell 2000, 17). In the reverse direction, in 1920 the number of US-born living in Canada was about 4 percent as large as was the total US-resident population, dropping to slightly more than 1 percent by 1990. Thus border effects for migration have grown substantially over the past century, coincident with the rise of the importance of the nation-state. No doubt some of the decline of international migration between the two countries has been due to policies in both countries controlling the pace and structure of immigration; but these periodic changes in policy cannot easily explain the long downward trend in international mobility between the two countries. There have been periods of higher mobility over the century, with net migration north during the Vietnam War period, large southbound movements of professionals during the 1950s and 1960s, and much talk in Canada during the late 1990s of new southbound flows. As will be noted in Chapter 2, the 1990s data provide scant support for this talk.

The second relevant strand of the migration literature documents the importance of networks as a determinant of the scale and patterns of migration, and it demonstrates the importance of migration to subsequent patterns of trade, investment, and migration. Migrants follow established pathways because those who precede send back information about possibilities and prospects, provide contacts for newcomers, and offer a community into which to settle upon arrival. Thus it is that there come to be dense pockets of migrants who originated in the same village many thousands of kilometres away. These clusters are more apparent, and denser, where the immigrants have come from further away and cross more linguistic, political, and cultural divides. Migrants bring more migrants in their wake, and the transnational networks they create generate, in turn, matching patterns of international trade and investment. For example, the country mix of immigrants to Canada helps to predict the pattern of subsequent changes in Canadian trade patterns with the countries of origin. These changes are more apparent for Canadian imports than exports, suggesting that at least part of the effect relates to the fact that many immigrants maintain their taste for goods from the home country (Head and Ries 1998).[7] The migration literature thus shows strong border effects while also illustrating that human migration both depends upon and provides international networks of information and support.

There is a burgeoning field of research into the scope, density, causes, and consequences of social norms and networks. Although such study goes back many years, within a number of disciplines and under a number of names, it has had a resurgence in the past decade under the heading "social capital." A recent OECD (2001, 41) report defines social capital as "networks together with shared norms, values and understandings that facilitate co-operation within or among groups." This encompasses almost exactly the same factors that I have suggested are important determinants of the density of trade and other economic and social interactions. If the evidence on social capital should show that the strength of networks generally decreases with distance and across national borders, then this would provide further support for the notion that differences in network densities explain differences in trade and other economic transactions.

One early piece of research into the effects of borders on networks was a study of the relative intensity of long-distance telephone calls between cities in Ontario, Quebec, and the United States. Using a gravity equation to model the expected effects of size and distance, the study (Mackay 1958) found that call frequencies were highest within the home province, lower between cities with different principal languages, and by far the lowest across the international boundary; the size and distance-adjusted intensity of calls was fifty times greater between Ontario cities than it was between Ontario and nearby US cities.

The path-breaking recent research into the nature and consequences of norms and networks by Putnam (1993) and his associates involves the long-term study of democracy in the various regions of modern Italy. Putnam was studying the efficiency of regional government and, especially, how it developed in different regions during the aftermath of 1980s reforms that devolved important powers onto regional governments. He collected numerous measures of the quality of norms and shared networks within the twenty regions and found that those regions with the highest quality of social capital delivered higher quality services to their citizens and made the best use of the newly devolved powers. Indeed, there is some evidence that their better use of these new powers was responsible for a reversal of what, in Italy, had been a replication of the Europe-wide postwar convergence of incomes per capita (Helliwell and Putnam 1995). Putnam found – and this is important for the study of international differences in norms and networks – that there were large and long-sustained inter-regional differences between norms and networks, despite large migration flows among the regions. However, for Italy, as for most other countries, most people stayed close to where they were born, and their networks and norms were similarly local.

When Putnam turned his research to the United States, he found that many measures of social capital had been growing for the first sixty years of the twentieth century and, thereafter, had been falling at about the same rate. Since his US and Italian researches had both shown that communities with high levels of his social capital measures tended to rank high on many indicators of economic, physical, and community welfare, he sounded widely heeded warnings about the possible risks to the fabric of US communities (Putnam 1995, 2000). The possible causes and, especially, the consequences of changes in the nature of social capital will be dealt with in Chapter 2. What I wish to note here is that Putnam discovered strong differences from state to state with regard to many of the measures of social capital. Earlier research (Almond and Verba 1963) on the quality of mid-century civic life found large differences among countries in many measures and consequences of social capital, especially with regard to levels of interpersonal trust. Three features of these international differences are to be noted here: (1) they persist for decades; (2) they are transported from one country to another in tandem with migrations; and (3) they are in some cases traceable to specific events or government policies. I document the long-standing nature of these differences in the next chapter, making use of World Values Survey measures spanning twenty years for as many as fifty countries (Inglehart et al. 2000). The extent to which these international differences are transported with migration has been studied by Rice and Feldman (1997), who found that a strong predictor of interstate differences in US interpersonal trust was differences in the number of residents whose parents or grandparents had been born in countries with high levels of trust. In the same vein, Putnam (2000) has found that one of the best predictors of interstate differences in trust levels is the share of the population with Scandinavian ancestors. To understand the latter point, one needs to know that measures of interpersonal trust are significantly higher in Scandinavian countries than elsewhere (see Chapter 2). Finally, Raiser's (1997) study of social capital in post-1990 Russia shows a link between trust levels and events, and Worms (2002) has shown a link between trust levels and policies, suggesting that the unusually low levels of interpersonal trust in France (relative to those in other OECD countries) may be partly due to the fact that pre- and postrevolutionary governments in that country systematically suppressed various non-state networks, seeing them as potential threats to the status and legitimacy of the state.

I have been arguing thus far that the quality of networks is an important determinant of many other forms of economic and social contact and that networks are much tighter close to home and in the same country. I made the latter point, in part, by showing the existence of long-sustained international and interstate differences in various measures of social capital. The existence of these differences may be sufficient to show that networks decay with distance and borders, but it is not necessary. For example, it is possible that several countries could show the same aggregate levels and distributions of various measures of social capital but still have networks that were largely unconnected with one another. Indeed, that is almost surely the case. However, study of the radius of trust and networks, and the extent to which individuals are involved in many different types of networks (for different purposes and with different implications for their behaviour and attitudes), is still in its infancy. Thus it is premature to draw firm conclusions about the extent to which various overlapping networks decay with distance and across borders. It is likely that changes in the types and patterns of communication, ranging from the jet plane in the 1960s to e-mail and the Internet in the 1980s and 1990s, are altering the nature and costs of developing and maintaining different types of network.

Turning to more formal institutions, there is ample evidence that these differ in both quality and features from country to country and, to a lesser extent, as one moves from one region to another within any given country. Kaufmann, Kraay, and Zoido-Lobatoni (1999a, 1999b) have compiled more than thirty measures of different aspects of the quality of national institutions, mainly focusing on the quality of government. They have found that international differences in average quality are large and have significant effects on economic growth. In Chapter 2, I present evidence showing that the quality of national institutions, as measured by the Kaufmann, Kraay, and Zoido-Lobatoni data, have significant effects on well-being beyond those flowing indirectly through economic growth and per capita incomes. For now, there are three points to register: (1) international institutional differences are significant; (2) they signal differences in the cost of and capacity for successful economic and social transactions; and (3) even if there were no international variations in the average quality of institutions, differences in their structure and details could lead to greater uncertainty and higher costs for those dealing in unfamiliar territory.

2 Checking National Well-Being

THIS CHAPTER IS ABOUT NATIONAL ECONOMIC AND SOCIAL POLICIES, AS was the second McLean Lecture, which I delivered in November 2000. Since I gave that lecture I have seen further possibilities for explaining and evaluating national policies through the systematic use of measures of well-being. In the original lecture I covered health care, social capital, education and research, taxation and the brain drain, inequalities and redistribution (including internal migration), and a range of macroeconomic issues, including whether Canada should have an independent monetary policy and exchange rate.[8] The common thread linking the discussion was based on the strong border effects identified in the first McLean Lecture. National economies and societies are separate enough that domestic policies can be quite different from those in neighbouring countries; consequently, they can be designed to meet domestic needs rather than foreign preferences.

One of the challenges I faced in presenting this broad range of issues in my original lecture was to find a way to make them coherent parts of an integrated assessment. I was then just beginning to see the full possibilities of using measures of subjective well-being for this purpose. Putnam (2000, Chap. 20) had already established links between measures of social capital and subjective well-being across US states and had subsequently combined individual-level and state-level data to get more accurate assessments of the importance of social capital (Putnam

2001). I immediately wondered if it might be possible to obtain comparable measures of subjective well-being from enough countries, and covering enough years, to provide a more comprehensive assessment of how individual-level and societal-level influences combine to shape well-being.

Putnam and I had already done something similar in our attempts to see whether the well-established links between education and social capital depended on how much education one had or, alternatively, on how much education one had relative to one's neighbours. Nie, Junn, and Stehlik-Barry (1996) had found that mutual trust depended positively on one's own education and also on national levels of education. By contrast, they found that, for some measures of participation in civic life, there were positive effects from one's own education but equally large negative effects from national education, implying that general increases in education would not raise these measures of community engagement. Our own results had been quite different, showing that both trust and participation depend positively both on one's own education level and on the average education in one's community. Subsequent statistical research revealed that the Nie, Junn, and Stehlik-Barry results altered so as to become consistent with ours if one used more precise measures of the average level of education in the community (Helliwell and Putnam 1999).

That result was interesting in its own right but was, I think, more important in suggesting a general approach to the separation of individual-level and community-level factors. One way of thinking about the appearance of community-level variables, once the appropriate individual-level influences have been taken into account, is as a way of estimating what economists call "externalities."

One simple example may help to clarify what is at stake. Suppose for a moment that the community is a better place for all if there are lots of reading groups. An equation estimating the likelihood of somebody being in a reading group depends positively on that person's own education. If that were the end of the story, then increases in general education would increase the number of people in reading groups because of the effect of each person's education on his or her chances of participating. Now suppose that we add the community average level of education to the equation. If it has no effect, then we would conclude that there are no external effects of education, at least through participation in reading groups. If it has a negative effect, then we would infer, as did Nie, Junn, and Stehlik-Barry, that to some extent participation depends on one's relative education, so that only the most educated in a community partici- pate. Any negative effect could be interpreted as a negative externality. If this negative community-level effect were as large as the positive individual-level effect, then the net effect of education would be relative, and general increases in education would have no effect on total partici- pation in reading groups. On the other hand, if community-level educa- tion contributes positively to the average person's likelihood of being in a reading group, then education has positive externalities. As you might guess, participation in reading groups is one of the cases where both one's own and community-level education levels have a positive effect. It does stand to reason that having more readers in one's neighbourhood is likely to produce more interesting possibilities for reading groups.

This particular example is not expected to cause anyone to jump up and down with the excitement of new discovery. However, the method used may also be generally applied to the assessment of the effects of policies and their external effects. Estimates of external effects are of tra- ditional importance to economists because they provide much of the rationale for community-level provision or support of services, ranging from education and health through public broadcasting, community cen- tres, and playing fields. Here was a method that could perhaps be of fairly wide application. But what was missing in our first application of the method was some direct measure of welfare beyond simply defining it as something that was presumed to be good for people. The missing link is provided by subjective measures of well-being as they offer at least the potential for measuring not just external effects from specific variables but also for integrating the effects of aspects of life as disparate as income and health.

When I finally realized the potential for using individual and community-level variables to determine subjective well-being, I uttered a conditional "Eureka" and set about to see whether it was a dream or a realistic possibility.[9] It would, at the least, require months of re-tooling because well-being has been systematically studied for decades in psychology and epidemiology, and for many centuries in philosophy and literature. On the practical side, nothing very ambitious could be done by way of evaluating institutions and social capital unless the sample of data were large enough to include many countries with quite different histories and institutions. Ideally, the data sample would also have to be long enough to assess trends in well-being. Only just over a year has passed since I saw the light clearly, so I am still in the fairly early days of my research. However, I was lucky enough to have eight clear months in which to work and to have had access to the exceptionally well-organized data files from the World Values Survey (WVS) (Inglehart et al. 2000).

My first step was to survey the related literature in psychology and epidemiology to find out the likely validity of the methodology and to build up an inventory of established results that would have to be replicated or otherwise tested within the global sample (Helliwell 2001b). I also found a resurgence of interest in well-being research among psychologists,[10] many of whom advocate directing a larger fraction of psychological research from illness to well-being since it had long been established in psychology (as well as in epidemiology) that illness and wellness are not simply two sides of the same coin.

There is also a large epidemiological literature showing strong linkages from family, friends, and community involvement to subsequent health outcomes.[11] This literature, surveyed in OECD (2001) and Helliwell (2001b), is especially important for its reminder that, whatever direct links may be found from social capital to subjective well-being, the total effects of social capital must be calculated to include those flowing indirectly through physical health to subjective well-being.

I also discovered, or rediscovered, a branch of the economic literature that has used measures of subjective well-being to compute the costs of unemployment (Clark and Oswald 1994; Oswald 1997); to estimate well-being trade-offs between inflation and unemployment (Di Tella, MacCulloch, and Oswald 2001); to study different attitudes towards inequality and the welfare state in the United States and Europe (Alesina, Di Tella, and MacCulloch 2001); and even to assess the well-being effects of differing governmental structures among Swiss cantons (Frey and Stutzer 2000). These and some other economic applications have been recently surveyed by Frey and Stutzer (2002).

On reflection, it is natural to interpret the United Nations Development Program (UNDP) measures of the quality of life, published and widely noticed each year, as another attempt to combine the level and distribution of economic, educational, and health outcomes to provide a more comprehensive measure of well-being. Quantitative well-being research offers a natural set of weights with which to combine these different aspects of life and society, and permits a larger range of factors and institutions to be brought into the assessment. In the absence of some evidence-based weighting system, those with differing values will be unable to agree on a common weighted measure of well-being. For example, the Fraser Institute (Emes and Hahn 2001) has argued that the UNDP's assumed utility function "arbitrarily" reduces the value attached to increases in per capita incomes. Its preferred measure of human progress, by contrast, treats each dollar increase in per capita incomes as having equal value, and adds a measure based on the numbers of televisions and telephones per capita, in the process putting the United States at the top of the 1999 well-being list and reducing Canada to sixteenth place. The UNDP measure for that year had Canada first, and the United States was behind a number of countries. The well-being data provide the possibility of using direct evidence to support the choice of weights in a well-being index as well as direct measures of well-being itself. As may be seen below, the debate between the Fraser Institute and the UNDP about the appropriate weight to attach to per capita incomes was settled very much on the side of the UNDP, with the estimated weight on higher national per capita incomes among the rich countries being even less than that implied by the UNDP measure.

Enough by way of introduction. The latest results from the research are reported elsewhere (Helliwell 2002b). In this chapter I emphasize those that are most germane to the assessment of the effects of national institutions and policies. The data sample includes almost 88,000 observations from three waves of the WVS: the first in the early 1980s, the second in the early 1990s, and the third in the late 1990s. Almost fifty countries are included, although they differ from wave to wave. Canada and several of the other OECD countries were not involved in the third wave. The mid-1990s wave did, however, involve thirty countries in total, of which eight had been members of the former Soviet Union (FSU) and seven were from Eastern Europe. The dependent variable being explained by the research is the answer, on a ten-point scale, given by individuals when asked to evaluate their general life satisfaction.[12] On average, people are satisfied with their lives, with a global average answer of 6.8 on a scale of 10. However, there are large differences among countries and regions. For example, the sample average value for well-being is 4.96 in FSU countries and 6.23 in Eastern Europe, compared to 7.72 in the United States, 7.86 in Canada, and 7.94 in the Scandinavian countries.

The purpose of the modelling is to see if individual and societal variables can be combined to explain differences in life satisfaction among individuals and among countries. The time periods and country groups are allowed to have separate constant terms to allow for time and country culture differences that are not captured fully by the variables included in the model.[13] There are several individual-level variables, and a smaller number of societal or national-level variables, used as independent variables. At the individual level, the variables include a subjective measure of physical health, age group, marital status, income by decile, whether one is unemployed, one's education level, and several individual measures of social capital and norms. These include the standard trust question,[14] whether one attends church once a week or more, whether God is very important to one's life, how many non-church community groups one is a member of, and whether one thinks that it is ever justifiable to cheat on taxes. The results replicate earlier research in showing strong positive well-being effects from the subjective state of physical health, marriage, and the avoidance of unemployment. They also match other research findings that show that, if separate allowance is made for health, income, marital status, and so on, there is a clearly defined U-shaped pattern for the age effect. Well-being is lower in the early forties than at either end of the age spectrum. It is higher for the over-sixty-fives than for those in the youngest age group (18-24). Well-being rises with one's relative income until one reaches the middle of the national income distribution, and then it tapers off. The effects of education are strongly positive when assessed on their own but largely fall out of the explanation when account is taken of the various explicit channels through which these effects are implemented. I'll return to this important part of the story later in more detail.

What are the individual-level effects of the networks and norms of social capital? Memberships, trust, and values all have separately important effects. Both aspects of religion – regular church-going and belief in the importance of God – are associated with significantly higher subjective well-being. The same is true for memberships in non-church community organizations. Turning to trust and values, subjective well-being is significantly higher for those who think that in general others can be trusted, and who think that it is never justifiable to cheat on taxes. The estimated effects are statistically strongly significant and large relative to the effects of income. For example, the combined effects of church-going and belief in God are almost as large as are those involved in moving from the very bottom to the top of the income distribution. And to believe that it is never right to cheat on taxes has the well-being equivalent of several deciles increase in relative income. These effects are all at the individual level, and they may be either augmented or reversed by those at the national level. Except in the case of income, positive effects from the national level variables provide evidence of positive externalities, or spillover effects. Income is different because the individual-level income variables are already expressed in relative terms, reflecting the nature of the survey data. This implies substantial negative externalities of income as one's well-being rises equally with a rise in one's own income or a fall in the national average income. Thus there is no increase in average well-being if all incomes rise at the same percentage, and there is a fall in average well-being if there is a change in the income distribution that increases inequality. This is because of the fact that well-being increases more from moving from the bottom to the middle than from the middle to the top of the income distribution. Despite the extensive documentation that increases in satisfaction from income are based more on relative than on absolute incomes, the results at the individual level are likely to represent too extreme a version of the relative income hypothesis.

Thus as we move to add national-level variables, we would expect to find that those living in richer countries have higher subjective well-being, at least for movements from poverty to some level of affluence, than do those living in poorer countries. This is indeed the case, although there are diminishing returns at play here as well. Moving from poverty to middle income levels, in terms of average national real GDP per capita, is matched by significant increases in national average well-being, but this effect diminishes thereafter and becomes insignificantly small at the top end of the world income distribution. When the individual- and national-level income effects are combined, there is evidence of negative externalities in the sense that increases in average national income, without any increase in one's own income, reduce one's reported life satisfaction in countries as rich as those in the OECD.[15]

By contrast, for the social capital variables, the external effects are generally positive. Higher average participation in community organizations is associated with higher subjective well-being, even among those whose own participation is unchanged. Similarly, to live in a high trust nation, or in a nation where others think that it is wrong to cheat on taxes, increases one's subjective well-being. Since these results are derived from an equation that already takes into account the individual's own trust and beliefs, they cannot simply reflect some unmeasured personality differences at the individual level. Thus these two-level results provide strong evidence of the positive well-being effects of living in societies with high levels of social capital. A final reminder: all of these effects of social capital are above and beyond the effects they may have flowing through health or incomes. The effects of social capital on health, and hence indirectly on well-being, have been long-studied and fully documented elsewhere.

Returning to education, the full model results show that there are no positive or negative externalities from living in nations with higher average levels of education, and the individual level results also show only small and sometimes insignificant effects. At first blush this seems a puzzling result as much of the research surveyed by the OECD (2001) shows high individual benefits from education and also reveals education levels to be among the strongest and most reliable predictors of the variables used as proxy measures for social capital. Would we thus not expect to find positive external effects from education? And perhaps also positive well-being effects from one's own education? Yet in the full model this is not apparent. Why? Because the full model also includes the main channels through which positive private and social effects are likely to be manifested. Indeed, one measure of the overall success of the model is that it so successfully explains the channels through which education has its positive effects on individual well-being that there is no remaining need for the inclusion of individual or national education levels.

To confirm that this comforting interpretation is plausible it is necessary to do some back-checking. The simplest way of checking is to include both individual and national education levels in a model that includes only the time and regional variables, and that excludes the income, social capital, and other variables that are thought to capture the channels through which education influences well-being. This has been done (Helliwell 2002b, equations 3 and 4), and the stripped-down equation does indeed show strong positive linkages from both individual and national education levels to subjective well-being. Education thus has strong individual well-being benefits as well as significant positive externalities. The full model results show that these effects flow through higher incomes, increased participation and trust, and better institutions that are facilitated by the higher levels of education.

What about the quality of institutions? In addition to the variables that have both individual and national average values, the model contains a variable designed to reflect the quality of national-level institutions and services. This is an average of the six indexes of governmental quality compiled by Kaufmann, Kraay, and Zoido-Lobatoni (1999a), each of which is in turn a composite of several other measures. Since corruption levels, the efficiency of bureaucracy, the honesty of elections, and the transparency of regulations are all influenced by the national average levels of trust, norms of honesty, and education levels already in the equation, and since in any event the well-being effects of better government might be expected to flow mainly through higher levels of GDP per capita, it would not be surprising if this variable did not show a significant effect on subjective well-being. Yet it does display a strongly significant positive effect, showing that countries managing to achieve a more honest and effective government than their other circumstances would have predicted – the governmental over-achievers, if you like – thereby provide a level of well-being for their citizens that is above and beyond what would be predicted by the well-documented effects (Kaufmann, Kraay, and Zoido-Lobatoni 1999b) flowing through higher levels of GDP per capita.

From these preliminary results, what can we conclude about

national policies and their effects on well-being? The first point, which is carried over from Chapter 1, is that there are large international differences in norms and networks. These differences provide a degree of international separation that gives national governments both the opportunity and the need to support and maintain high-quality norms and institutions.

The new evidence in this chapter strengthens the case by showing that the quality of norms and institutions has strong well-being effects even beyond the more extensively studied effects flowing through better health and higher incomes. Indeed, the well-being results show that it is misleading to concentrate exclusively on the effects flowing through productivity and incomes. This is because the non-economic channels are likely to be larger than are those flowing via productivity and incomes (e.g., Wolfe and Haveman 2001). In addition, the well-being equations suggest that the direct well-being effects of social capital are more sustained, and are more likely to be accompanied by positive externalities, than are the effects of higher incomes. The income effects, as has been seen, are largely relative in nature and, in any event, get smaller as incomes rise, thus tilting the evaluation ever more towards the quality of life rather than towards the levels of material standards of living as coun tries and individuals become more affluent.

It is important for governments, which have an essential role in the maintenance of so many aspects of the social fabric, to avoid needless or heedless damage to these institutions in pursuit of what is called international competitiveness, often sought for its presumed ability to deliver sustained growth in material standards of living. The evidence of this chapter cautions that a balanced evaluation of policies requires a much wider and richer canvas – one that takes full account of the sources of well-being. If some aspects of globalization threaten some non-economic aspects of society, then these risks should be evaluated before rather than after the damage has occurred. Getting the eggs together again, and back in the basket, is no mean feat; and this is demonstrated as graphically in contemporary Russia as it is in the nursery rhyme where all the king's horses and all the king's men struggled with the remains of Humpty Dumpty.

What are some of the possible implications for specific policies? My general point is that geography and borders matter, and that geographic and political separations are likely to reflect current and continuing differences in values and preferences. Thus it is desirable to have education, health, social and other domestic policies that reflect domestic preferences. The continuing economic separation of nation-states is substantial enough to make this possible. To take a specific example that is much discussed, it has been frequently argued that there has been a large increase in skilled migration from Canada to the United States and that this imposes the need to match US tax and redistribution policies in order to offset the outflows (Iqbal 1999). However, closer inspection of the data shows skilled southbound migration to be much smaller than widely believed and much smaller than it has been in previous decades (Frank and Bélair 1999; Helliwell 1999; Zhao, Drew, and Murray 2000; Helliwell and Helliwell 2000, 2001; Finnie 2001), and detailed analysis of the tax effects show that, while taxes do significantly influence migration decisions, the total effects of even quite large tax differences are surprisingly small (Wagner 2000; Helliwell 2000, 23). The constraints on the abilities of societies to design policies to match their own preferences may be based more on perceptions than on reality. If so, then these perceptions need to be changed before the ability to design domestic policies can be used effectively. Just as the extent to which national societies and economies are distinct from one another is largely underestimated, so is the case for national autonomy.

The well-being evidence reported above shows that both health and education have substantial direct and indirect effects at both the individual and community levels. These external effects, which have long provided the rationale for government support for health and education, are large enough, and contrast strongly enough with the corresponding effects of higher individual incomes, to suggest that protection of high standards of health care and education is worth what it takes to do well. The fact that trust in government is even more threatened than is interpersonal trust suggests that governments attempting to meet demands and expectations for higher quality health, education, knowledge creation, public finance, and social safety nets must recognize that their own credibility needs to be rebuilt simultaneously. This will be no mean feat, but it is simplified by the general advice to first heed local and national preferences and opportunities.

The fact that globalization has not destroyed, or even strongly diminished, the scope and need for national policies does not mean that change is not taking place. Even if changes were slight there is no assurance that the policies in place suit current circumstances, let alone those of the coming decades. The general case can be made that national fiscal and monetary policies continue to have largely national effects and are not excessively constrained by policy choices elsewhere. International experiences are important for the lessons they may teach about what works and what does not (taking due account of the fact that societal differences alter what can work as well as what is desired). For developing countries, with more choices yet to be made, with more examples to consider, and more institutions to be built, the problems are at once starker and more difficult than they are for developed countries. What institutions should they be trying to emulate and how best could other countries help them to succeed? What global frameworks would help them most and what can the richer and more established countries do to help? How, for a country like Canada, should these global issues be squared with policies designed in the national interest? And what, after all, would the latter look like in today's world? These are the questions for Chapter 3.

3 Combining National and Global Well-Being

THIS CHAPTER, LIKE THE LECTURE UPON WHICH IT IS BASED, ADDRESSES international issues from a Canadian perspective or, perhaps more accurately, from several Canadian perspectives. To help make the issues more concrete, I shall define and assess alternative strategies. What package of national and international polices might best serve Canada and the world as a whole? I shall first consider explicitly national and then international policies, and discuss two alternative policy strategies.

National Fiscal and Monetary Policies

The general tenor of the discussion in the preceding chapters is that national economies are separate enough that there is still lots of scope for choosing national fiscal and monetary policies. But that does not settle the specifics. What sort of monetary and exchange rate policy is to be preferred? What constraints do monetary policies impose on fiscal policies? The logic of the Euro, and of the Maastricht Treaty (which established the conditions for countries that wish to adopt the Euro as their national currency), is that belonging to a common currency area requires a fairly tight convergence of monetary and fiscal policies. In this vein, the Irish government was recently chastised by the European Commission for adopting an excessively expansionary fiscal policy that, it was thought, might threaten the stability of the Euro. The idea that a common currency covering many countries requires them to follow the same fiscal policy, within fairly narrow limits, sounds puzzling to Canadian ears since Canadian provinces have always shared a common currency and fiscal policies have varied much from one province to another. The attitude in the provinces, and even in the federal government, has generally been that the costs of excessive provincial debt would be borne by the taxpayers of the profligate provinces, with no attendant threat either to the national currency or to monetary policy. If the pattern of policies chosen, however, results in inflation rates that are very different from one part of the country to another, then there are resulting complications for the design of national monetary policy. However, the constraint lies chiefly in the requirement, or hope, that the fiscal policies of the regions will alleviate rather than exacerbate differences in macroeconomic balance among the provinces.

There are, in addition, two major reasons why regionally differentiated fiscal policies are less likely to be required in Canada than among the countries in the Euro zone. The first, already emphasized, is that trade, capital mobility, and migration are several times greater among Canadian provinces than they are among EU countries, thus ensuring a faster movement of resources from one province to another in response to different macroeconomic balances. The second is that the Canadian system of equalization payments and the large established national safety net system (especially Employment Insurance for individuals and equalization payments for provincial governments) imply much greater inter-regional transfers of resources than are available in the EU. These transfers function to maintain incomes and consumption in regions that are cyclically or even secularly depressed. Indeed, these transfer systems are so extensive as to lead some commentators to believe that they hamstring incentives to interprovincial mobility and prolong or forestall necessary adjustments. Within this context it is perhaps surprising, and certainly reassuring, that interprovincial mobility in Canada is, if anything, more fluid than is interstate mobility in the United States. It is also more responsive to differences in incomes and employment (Helliwell 1996a), despite the much greater extent of interprovincial redistribution in Canada.

Thus Canadian provinces are freer to make their own fiscal policy decisions than are the national governments bound by the conditions of the Maastricht Treaty, while the much greater extent of interprovincial mobility and redistribution means that there is less need for additional fiscal adjustment at the level of the provincial governments. I think that while the requirement of fiscal convergence may have been a suitable way of ensuring the seriousness of macroeconomic resolve among governments wanting to gain the monetary credibility that was expected to be provided by the Euro, it does not seem to be a necessary continuing feature of national fiscal policies among countries sharing a common currency. Indeed, in the light of the much more limited mobility and much smaller cross-border fiscal transfers in the EU, there is more need for independent national fiscal polices there than in Canada's provinces. Since the EU countries gave up their monetary policy independence upon adopting the Euro as their national currency, there is even more need to have some fiscal freedom to combat regional disturbances. I should caution, however, that the advantages of fiscal policy freedom at the regional level or national level are based on the premise that they will be used appropriately to offset rather than to exacerbate macroeconomic disturbances. If one were sceptical of any such policy scope being used appropriately, for either political or technical reasons, then there would be no macroeconomic grounds for leaving fiscal policy freedom at the national or provincial levels. There would still remain, however, fundamental issues relating to provision of public services, the nature of redistribution through taxes and transfers, and the means used to pay for public services.

Monetary and Exchange Rate Policy

It is common to say that a country can have either a monetary policy or a fixed exchange rate but not both. In fact, the extent to which international markets are segregated is such that there is more scope, at least in the short run, for combining the two than this stark choice would seem to suggest. In the last fifty years most countries have had systems somewhere in the middle. For example, countries with pegged exchange rates have occasionally changed their peg values and have usually had some margins of variation about these values. On the other hand, countries with flexible exchange rates have often designed their domestic monetary policies by taking some account of the external value of their currency. With the breakdown of the Bretton Woods system of pegged exchange rates in the early 1970s, exchange rates among the main industrial currencies became flexible, with the European Monetary System limiting fluctuation among the currencies belonging to its exchange rate mechanism. At the beginning of 1999 a new European currency – the Euro – was introduced. This marked the first major move towards the use of a common currency among advanced industrial countries.

There has been much speculation about the likely effects of the Euro on trade, growth, and macroeconomic policy design. It is too early for definitive evidence on that score, but time should tell, since there are three major members of the EU which have not adopted the Euro – the United Kingdom (UK), Denmark, and Sweden – with Denmark nonetheless maintaining a fixed exchange rate with the Euro. Thus it should be increasingly feasible to separate the trade effects of exchange rate fixity from those of currency union and free trade areas. Early studies of real exchange rate variability on trade found them to be very small.[16] More recently, Andrew Rose (2000) has used bilateral trade data for a large sample of countries to estimate the effects of exchange rate fixity separately from those of having a common currency. He concluded that countries using the same currency were likely to trade three times more with each other than they would have done otherwise, above and beyond the more limited effects of having fixed exchange rates. In partial justification of what he and others regard as very high effects of currency unions on trade, he noted that, since international border effects for trade had already been found to be very large, it was perhaps plausible to think of one-third of the effect as being due to using different currencies. However, this would imply, implausibly, that trade between the Netherlands and France will treble relative to the trade between Denmark and France after whatever adjustment period there may be.

The main criticisms of the Rose result have been based on the fact that the bulk of the cases he studied relate to currency unions between individual larger countries and numerous small dependencies (e.g., between the United States and Panama, and between New Zealand and several small Pacific Islands), where there are many other reasons beyond the common currency to expect trade to be greater than average. Indeed, these reasons, some of which Rose tries to account for, probably lie behind both the currency union and the trade, without the former having been the cause of the latter. To get more convincing data, it is necessary, but difficult, to find cases where currency unions have been formed or broken with as little else as possible remaining unchanged. The Euro example, with the UK, Denmark, and Sweden as control cases, is thus a valuable example.

Thom and Walsh (2001) have studied the 1979 abandonment of the Irish-UK common currency union as a completed test case, and they can find no discernible effect of the currency union. Subsequent trade between the two countries evolved at the same rate after the break as before. They explain the difference between their results and those of Rose as being due to the special features of the small dependencies that make up such a large part of the Rose sample. They argue that the UK-Irish case is the only one involving developed industrial countries on both sides and that, hence, it provides the most relevant basis for assessing the trade effects for industrial countries thinking of the consequences of joining the Euro or adopting some other national currency as their own. I am more convinced by the Thom and Walsh evidence than by the less applicable Rose estimates and am hence inclined to assume the trade effects of currency unions to be modest, unless the experience of the Euro should prove the contrary. There is thus far no significant sign of weakening trade and capital linkages between Euro and non-Euro members of the EU relative to those among Euro members, but time will tell.

In the absence of trade creation, which Rose and van Wincoop (2001) argue to be the most important consequence of currency unions, the main effects reflect some trade-off between potential savings in currency exchange costs and the loss of ability to make monetary policy to meet domestic circumstances. Most model-based estimates of both the savings and the macroeconomic costs of the loss in monetary independence are fairly modest, with the net effect being smaller still.

Does the Logic of the Euro Apply to North America?

In Canada the issue of exchange rate policy has been much discussed in the wake of the launch of the Euro.[17] This is in some sense puzzling since most countries are attracted by fixed exchange rates in general, and common currencies in particular, as a means of acquiring, or re-acquiring, monetary credibility. Thus Argentina was attracted into adopting a rigid currency board linkage with the United States dollar in order to eliminate entrenched inflationary expectations. Canada, by contrast, had been among the first countries to move to inflation targeting as an explicit monetary policy objective and, during the 1990s, had one of the lowest and most stable inflation rates among the industrial countries. Indeed, restrictive monetary policy has regularly been argued to be a major cause of Canada's relatively sluggish growth performance during the 1990s (Fortin 1999, 2001). Some have argued that the price paid for low and stable inflation was too high; but the price has already been paid, and evidence from long-term interest rates suggests that, if anything, Canada's expected inflation rate lies below that for the United States.

If the reasons for revisiting the issue of exchange rate policy were not primarily macroeconomic, then what were they? To some extent they were probably a reflex reaction to the formation of the Euro: if there is a movement under way towards regional currencies, then countries need to join one of the ships or risk being left behind. This reason is more likely to have been appropriate at the time of the launch of the Euro. Two years later – especially in light of the subsequent Danish vote not to join, the continuing debate in the UK, and the emergence of disputes about the extent to which Euro memberships should impose fiscal straightjackets on national governments – the Euro is more easily seen as being more political than economic in its origins.

It is easier now to see that, for many countries, both the economic and the political logic of the Euro is particular to the broader EU project and not easily exportable to other countries or regions. It needs to be remembered that the preceding EU exchange rate mechanism was a fairly rigid peg to the German mark. This meant that, effectively, German monetary policy became EU monetary policy for committed members of the exchange rate mechanism. They had to mimic German policy, and yet, in key cases (e.g., France), they were still paying a long-term interest rate premium, reflecting market doubts that the strong-franc policy would be maintained under pressure. Thus for France, which was committed to the exchange rate mechanism and to a tighter Europe in general, the Euro idea provided a double benefit – lower interest rates plus greater national control over monetary policy (since France would be represented directly in Euro monetary policy decisions). For Italy, the Euro offered a slightly riskier but potentially higher payoff – riskier because inflation was more deeply embodied in expectations (and even as a source of public finance) and higher because successful adoption of the Euro would achieve monetary stability plus some role in the design of European monetary policy. For the smaller countries, the balance of arguments depended on their circumstances. For Belgium and the Netherlands, monetary and expected exchange rate stability were already in place and European-level decision making well accepted, so the shift of monetary policy authority up to the European level was seen as a benefit compared to the loss of future monetary policy freedom. It should be noted that, in all countries except Denmark, the assessments were made by governments rather than by voters, with the general public, according to surveys, being more attached to their national currencies. This is especially the case for Germany, where in any case the Euro represented a loss of national sovereignty. For other countries previously attached to the Deutsche Mark (DM), adoption of the Euro led to an increase in national power over monetary policy, while for Germany the reverse was the case. The German government was willing to give up national autonomy, and to accept a monetary policy less attuned to German needs, in order to help eliminate any risk of a repeat of the wars that fractured Europe, and Germany itself, during the twentieth century.

As for the economics of the Euro, the trade creation effects remain to be seen. On the macroeconomic side, there is similar uncertainty about the likelihood of situations where countries will feel seriously hampered by the absence of control over domestic interest rates. The Irish situation has been noted as a case where tighter money, with or without a higher exchange rate, would have helped to offset emerging inflation. As already noted, international mobility of goods, services, capital, and population among the Euro countries is much less than it is among the provinces of Canada. The same is true for fiscal redistribution. All of these are factors used to define cases where common currencies may be optimal. The economic case for the Euro is thus less strong than it was seen to be by those who presumed higher degrees of international mobility than in fact exist. Experience under the Euro will help to show how much of the greater interprovincial mobility is due to the Canadian dollar itself.

How does the European experience relate to Canada? On the economic front, I have already presented evidence showing that Canada and the United States are much less likely to represent an optimal common currency area than is the EU. Although the EU has much less community-level redistribution and mobility than is evident among the Canadian provinces, there is still more of both within the EU than there is between Canada and the United States. Nor would adoption of the US dollar, with the accompanying monetary policy set by the US Federal Reserve, be a means of acquiring a lower or more stable inflation rate. This is because over the past decade Canadian inflation has been lower than US inflation.

Another economic criterion for countries wishing to share a common currency relates to exposure to common shocks. Here too there is more commonality of external shocks among Euro members than in Canada and the United States. The well-known reason for this is that Canada is much more specialized in raw materials than is the United States and is hence more likely to face terms-of-trade shocks when there are global swings in the prices of raw materials. These are more easily digested by the economy if the exchange rate is allowed to move so as to help absorb their effects. Market pressures and policies combine to produce this result under a flexible Canadian exchange rate, but they would not be able to do so if the Canadian dollar were tied to that of the US dollar.

The same issue arises to some extent even within the Canadian economy as the more resource-intensive western provinces find their resource booms more accentuated than they would be if there were a separate currency for western Canada. On the other hand, a manufacturing-based boom creates inflationary pressures mainly in Ontario and Quebec, especially if it is driven by high US output and inflation. This regional asymmetry of shocks imposes competing demands on national monetary policy because monetary restraint may be indicated for some regions but not for others. The Bank of Canada, which is required to set national interest rates in what the evidence shows to be a truly national capital market, balances these competing requirements to produce a policy that attaches some weight to all regional needs. But if Canada were to adopt the US dollar, then US monetary policy would continue to be set with US inflation and employment as the targets. And Canadian needs would necessarily receive a zero weight.

What of the political aspects? Here too there is little parallel between the North American and European cases, and the comparisons all suggest that it was more logical for Europe to invent the Euro than it would be for Canada to adopt the US dollar. The Euro was adopted within a European political structure that, for more than forty years, had been developing European-level laws, regulations, bureaucracies, and governments. Thus the idea of creating a new European-level central bank to set monetary policy for the Euro established no new precedents. In a sense, the European Central Bank (ECB) could be thought of as an institution for acquiring monetary powers for an already powerful and legitimized European government. It is true, however, that the ECB is generally independent of the European Commission and the European Parliament, having its powers and directors determined mainly by national governments of the member countries. Nonetheless, for member countries the ECB is simply another European-level institution with a specific mandate. Since most national governments had already been moving towards systems of governance that gave central banks substantial independence (with the aim of increasing the credibility of their efforts to control inflation), to transfer the task to a supranational institution involved little or no loss of national sovereignty. Indeed, as has been noted, many of the countries in the pre-Euro exchange rate mechanism had already ceded their powers over monetary policy, albeit on a retrievable basis, to the German central bank. For these countries the move to an ECB with direct board and management representation from their own country represented an increase in national sovereignty. For Germany the case is the reverse, and there was a definite transfer of sovereignty upward to the European level.

Is this European political situation mirrored in North America? Not at all, since there are no North-American-level governance or administrative structures with supranational powers. Thus the idea of a North American monetary union, with a North American central bank setting monetary policy, would require an unprecedented upward transferral of sovereignty by the United States. The transfer of monetary power by Germany was much smaller, was made in the pursuit of a larger political objective, and was seen within the context of many existing European-level institutions and powers. Since there is no political or economic constituency within the United States supporting such a transfer, any move towards a currency to be used jointly by Canada and the United States would in all likelihood involve the adoption of the US dollar as legal tender in Canada.

Within the European context the adoption of a European money to replace a national money is preferred by those who want to transfer sovereignty upwards and to create a stronger federal Europe with an increasing range of what are usually seen as national powers. This lies behind much of the political appeal to European voters – the chance to construct a Europe bigger than the United States and able to act as a counterweight in world affairs.

Within the Canadian context, adoption of the US dollar would be a straight horizontal transfer of sovereignty, passing control of Canadian monetary policy to a US Federal Reserve System that has no great desire to have such responsibilities and would certainly not be able to be accountable to Canadians. The usual political arguments for transferring control of monetary policy to a body that exists outside the normal political process are (1) to ensure that monetary policy decisions are made for the long-term benefit of citizens and (2) to ensure that the option of using the printing press to finance public spending is not easily available to governments. Implicit within such logic is the notion that the monetary authority is democratically and morally responsible to the citizens of the country, sharing their objectives and attempting to act in their best interests. To transfer this responsibility to another country's central bank, which is responsible to its own citizens, may provide independence from short-term national political control, but in the process it throws the baby out with the bathwater. In terms of governance, such a transfer would be dysfunctional.

What are the conditions under which adoption of the US dollar might nonetheless have some political appeal? One, which I have already discounted, is that Canadian monetary policy requirements should exactly align with those of the United States so that abdication of local control could save effort and still reach the right destination, much like drafting in a bicycle race. But aside from the general reasons to suppose that Canada and the United States do not form an optimal currency area, the history of past movements of the Canadian and US dollars have been such as to suggest that exchange rate flexibility has in fact acted to cushion Canada from external shocks. This is not widely recognized in Canada because there is a widespread tendency in the media to report the value of the Canadian dollar only in relation to that of the US dollar. This has the paradoxical consequence of the Canadian dollar being described as weakening when it is actually strengthening in relation to almost every currency except the US dollar. In circumstances like those of the last twenty years, where the US dollar has been perhaps the most volatile of all major currencies, the Canadian dollar has tended to follow suit but to a lesser extent, thus cushioning the Canadian economy from some of the costs of, for example, the strengthening of the US dollar in the first half of the 1980s and its decline in the second half. Hence the economic case for borrowing US monetary policy has little basis in the recent history of either exchange rates or inflation.

A second reason why one might favour the Canadian adoption of the US dollar is as part of a strategy to bring Canada more completely under the US umbrella, perhaps with an eye to eventually reacquiring some regional democratic control by applying for statehood. This would at least remove the democratic deficit by providing seats as well as shelter inside the US tent. Some of the reasons advanced for this have included historical inevitability; desire to acquire US levels of GDP per capita; and a belief that, in the absence of effective world-level rules and institutions, it is better to be part of the most powerful team than to be an independent player.

It is also possible that some people have an extreme form of nominal parity illusion, thinking that adopting the US dollar would automatically mean that their incomes in Canadian dollars would immediately be worth the same in US dollars. Certainly some people are already ignorant enough of purchasing power parity that they use the current market exchange rate when comparing real incomes in the two countries and also assume that it would provide the basis for adoption of the US dollar. Since the purchasing power parity rate is not far from halfway between the current market rate and the nominal parity rate of Cdn$1 = US$1, the two views are equally untenable. If the Canadian dollar were pegged to the US dollar at current rates, and especially if the peg were made irrevocable, it is inevitable that inflation in Canada over the next decade would be higher than that in the United States, whatever policy were adopted by the US Federal Reserve.

What of the view that, in light of rising trade with the United States, adoption of the US dollar is inevitable? Rising relative trade with the United States during the 1990s was a direct consequence of the Canada-US FTA and the later NAFTA. Just as the US-Canada Auto Pact of 1965 led to a rising trade share with the United States followed by stability, and just as the creation of each stage of the EU has had similar adjustment effects, so there is every reason not to extrapolate recent changes into the future. Indeed, the gravity model evidence more or less guarantees that any closing of the income and openness gaps between rich and poor countries will mean that an increasing fraction of world GDP and trade will take place outside North America, implying that, over the next fifty years, Canadian trade with overseas countries will grow faster than will Canadian trade with the United States. Even if the income gaps are slow to close, the increasing openness of the developing countries will make their trade an increasing share of the world total.

If increasing trade dependency on the United States is neither inevitable nor likely, then what else might make adoption of the US dollar inevitable? One view is that there might be an increasing move towards currency blocs, perhaps increasing the exposure of smaller countries that try to use either loosely fixed or flexible exchange rates in such a world. An extreme form of such opinions would be a world currency, and better to see this possibility early than late. What is the substance of such views? There is certainly a widespread view, appearing in newspapers as well as in the professional literature in the wake of the Asian currency crises of the late 1990s and of the increasing prevalence of the risks of contagion from one crisis to another, that it is increasingly difficult to have an exchange rate system in the middle ground between common currencies (or some other form of high-commitment fixing, such as a currency board) and flexible exchange rates. It is true (Fischer 2001) that there has been some hollowing out of the middle ground, but this has been marked by moves to flexible exchange rates more than by moves to more rigid exchange rates. This is especially true for those countries not involved in the Euro, for which the logic and explanations are special and, as I have argued above, are not applicable to the Canadian case. Thus even the hollowing out of the middle ground does not herald a general move towards rigidly fixed exchange rates but, rather, a redistribution of some of the middle-ground systems to the more polar versions.

If there is no political or economic inevitability, or even desirability, associated with Canadian adoption of the US dollar, then why is it currently being advocated? I think the most likely source of support comes from those who favour political and economic convergence of Canadian policies and institutions with US ones. For some, the adoption of the US dollar represents a logical next step in the process started by the Canada-US FTA, just as was feared by nationalist groups at the time of the FTA but was generally dismissed by economists interested primarily in a lowering of trade barriers. Indeed, much of the political and economic support for the FTA came from those who would have preferred to increase the openness of multilateral trade and who saw the FTA as a second-best strategy for attaining this, valuable chiefly to the extent it might serve as a pattern for changes at the global level. Obviously this sort of reasoning does not extend to adoption of the US dollar. Although the main support for adoption of the US dollar may come from those firms or individuals who want to move under the US economic and political umbrella, there may also be strategic support from those who think that, with an independent currency, Canadian monetary policy is likely to be too tight and Canadian interest rates too high. Business support for a common currency is especially likely to be forthcoming from firms operating in both countries and seeing any reduction in transactions costs as a net gain for them. Some of this support may be accepting of the macroeconomic and political implications, while other support may focus only on the costs. This is especially likely to be the case for Canadian firms already controlled from US head offices. On the other side of the debate, in Canada just as in the UK, some of the support for maintaining a national currency is based as much on the symbolism as on the economic and political significance of a national currency.

To more thoroughly evaluate the argument that favours a common currency as part of a general strategy of completing the North American economic and political space, it is necessary to consider it within a broader context. I shall do this by treating the adoption of a common currency as part of a larger strategy of forging deepening links with the United States relative to those with the rest of the world. Naturally, to a large extent the linkages between Canada and other countries can be considered and improved on a bilateral basis, with improvements in one not being at the expense of the other. But there are other places where a more global strategy would conflict with a North American strategy, and I shall also try to clarify the nature of these choices. I shall start by spelling out what an appropriate global strategy might look like for a country such as Canada and then consider what its implications might be for bilateral relations with the United States and vice versa.

Facing South or Facing Out? Bilateral or Multilateral?

What does the evidence on globalization suggest by way of advice for individuals, firms, national governments, and international organizations? Markets and societies are very different from region to region and from nation to nation. It is this fact, much more than border restrictions or fluctuating exchange rates, that keeps trade in goods and services much more local than transport costs or tariff rates would suggest. There is an equilibrium between the higher costs and risks of doing business in unfamiliar surroundings and the gains from specialization and comparative advantage. This trade-off has resulted in highly localized trade, even in a world widely regarded as globalized. The reasons for this localization are likely to include diminishing returns to trade that is increasingly adding to product variety rather than exploiting large differences in comparative advantage, coupled with the high costs and risks of operating in unfamiliar and often untrustworthy territory.

Networks and common norms, often described as social capital, underlie successful interactions of all types, ranging from trade and investment to foreign aid, social tolerance, and democratic reforms. These networks are fuelled by mutual trust, abetted by common institutions, and lubricated by frequent interactions. All of these decline with distance and as national borders are crossed. Although changing costs and technologies have radically altered the scope for long-distance and transborder linkages, the scale of these is still dwarfed by the density of local contacts and commerce. It is important to note that common cause and common values provide the basis for successful networks so that when these transcend distance and borders the density of contacts, and often of trade, will quickly follow suit.

Since the density and importance of local networks are often unrecognized, individuals, firms, and governments may be deluded into thinking that their customs, values, products, or policies will be as applicable far away, or even abroad, as they are at home. This may help to explain why foreign investors are the last ones into a local boom and the first ones out: their expectations and operations are based more in shared market perceptions, which are often volatile, than they are in detailed knowledge of the prospects and pitfalls of markets far from home. When people do not understand each other's values and institutions, they are more likely to be at cross-purposes and less likely to be mutually satisfied by their dealings.

How best to deal with these realities, if such they be? First, investment in knowledge, and prior establishment of reliable contacts, is likely to be valuable insurance. Second, acquisition of reliable knowledge and contacts takes time and effort, and favours patience, small scale, and investors with long time horizons. It is also likely to mean that the most robust international linkages are likely to be those that have strong roots in both countries, which means a much more pluralistic and diverse structure of management control. The evidence in Chapter 2 shows that trust and high-quality institutions have direct linkages to well-being. They also foster more efficient commercial exchanges, so that individuals and firms are both well advised to choose countries and contracts accordingly. Investing for the long term provides the opportunity and the responsibility for firms to take their communities and their institutions more seriously. In the case of foreign investors, this does not mean importing norms and values from the home country but, rather, respecting local norms while aiding local efforts to improve trust and to raise the quality of institutions in ways that reflect local needs and values.

What are the likely implications for the structure of relations between national governments, for the structure of foreign aid, and for the agendas of international organizations? For relations between national governments there seems much to be learned from sharing experiences in order to help build a stronger base for domestic policies. Although the evidence presented here of the great diversity of national societies may seem to make it hard to find transportable lessons, this very variety makes it possible to identify some channels of influence that might otherwise remain hidden. Each individual country might have made several changes simultaneously and be unable to disentangle their separate effects. Where there are many countries, each with different backgrounds and different evolutions of policy, there is a much greater chance of working out effective strategies. The variety of experiences means that most policy alternatives under consideration have been tried somewhere else. Careful analysis of these experiences should at least provide a helpful list of dos and don'ts. These lessons are especially important in institutional design and in providing warnings of consequences that may be hard to reverse. There is lots of evidence that mutual trust can take a long time to establish but be rapidly broken down. This asymmetry raises the value of learning from the mistakes and misfortunes of others.

With regard to foreign aid, the importance and the international variety of actual and possible future institutions means that it is likely to be most effective if it helps to unleash domestic capacities to govern and build. The right sorts of capacity building are likely to be more effective than cash but trickier to design and deliver. It is at least as important for capacity-building aid as for cash aid that it be untied. For capacity building this means that the blind application of one country's system in another country's system may well be as short sighted as is giving monetary aid tied to sales of one's own surplus production. A variety of channels may be necessary to deliver untied capacity building, including education and training, short-term secondments in both directions, and the design and application of technologies most appropriate to the skills and problems of the country receiving the aid. Social capital considerations suggest that these transfers are easiest to achieve where the motives of both parties are above suspicion and where considerations of geo-political power are out of the picture. This gives the edge to smaller advanced countries as aid providers because they can more easily be dealt with on an issue-by-issue basis and are less likely to have a larger political agenda to pursue. Geo-political aspects of aid are less apparent now than during the Cold War period, but aid recipients still find it easier to ask for and accept aid where they expect fewer strings to be attached.

What are the implications of the foregoing for the external policies of a middle-sized country like Canada? Canada is a middle power in more than size and heft: it also lies between Europe and the US, and between Asia and the US, in a number of policy dimensions. Canada shares with the Nordic countries the strongest commitments to international rules-based solutions to international problems, and it has equally strong commitments to delivering untied foreign aid in forms that are of most use to the recipients. It shares with these same countries a strong commitment to social safety nets (Blank and Hanratty 1993) and a variety of other institutional differences that make inequalities in income (Lemieux 1993; Gottschalk and Smeeding 1997) and health (Ross et al. 1999; Wolfson et al. 1999; Wolfson and Murphy 2000) much less stark in Canada than in the United States, even if more stark than in the Nordic countries. What follows are further reflections of Canada's midway position between Europe and the United States.

APEC, Seattle, Genoa: The Public Politics of Globalization

From the evidence presented in Chapters 1 and 2, globalization seems as much hype as reality – a slow-moving process that has increased international interdependence but has left nation-states and local communities with their basic capacities intact. This conclusion has an almost otherworldly air when juxtaposed with the debates and protests about globalization. Are the debates based on false perceptions or do they represent a foreshadowing of fundamental issues that are bound to become of greater importance? Some of each, I should think. The part of the debate most clearly based on false perceptions can perhaps best be characterized as having, on the one side, multinational corporations and perhaps some chambers of commerce and ministries of trade and industry and, on the other side, anti-capitalist-roaders. In this crude characterization, fuelled as much by what such groups say about each other as by how they would describe themselves, globaphiles are convinced that universal market openness is the single vital key to higher living standards. Globaphobes (Burtless et al. 1998), by contrast, regard globalization as the tool multinational corporations are using to rob the world's poor by exploiting their labour, resources, and environments; destroying their culture; and commanding their vassal governments to implement whatever laws and trade agreements would make these transfers easier to achieve.

From an extreme globaphile's perspective, some combination of multinational direct investment and open impersonal markets would permit the best of technology to be available everywhere and would give each individual and family the chance to prosper as never before. The extreme globaphobe would inevitably be pessimistic about the powers of democratic governments to control or reverse these forces and might therefore be inclined towards despair or even anarchy. This description of the globalization debate leaves much room in the middle, and that is probably where most opinions, although not most slogans, are to be found. If the evidence I have presented in Chapters 1 and 2 were widely known and accepted, then both of the extreme views described above would be seen to be without much support. Both positions assume much less, and less long-lasting, diversity than the world exhibits. But the evidence is generally not known, or is interpreted differently, so that both of the extreme views are frequently heard. But the middle ground is where realism lies, and where discussion should centre.

The middle ground contains the views of many of those protesting in the streets, those working behind closed doors in negotiations, and the general public reading the news with some mix of puzzlement and exasperation. Why exasperation? Readers may be exasperated because they share many of the worries of the globaphobes yet see their methods as crippling the sorts of international efforts that could serve to deliver more equity and opportunity to the world's poor. These readers understand that, if there are to be any solutions, then they must be delivered by democratic means; and open government is most at risk where chaos reigns. They also see that polarization begets more polarized views as each faction sees and exploits reports of fresh excesses by the other side.

How does social capital play into the process? It is possible to see the growing tide of protest, and the difficulties faced by national governments and international organizations trying to respond to it, as evidence of a lack of international social capital. In the absence of networks and norms that are shared across borders, it is easy to assume that what comes from afar comes with evil intent. This is too simple a story since, as has often been noted, what commonly makes a protest movement so tactically efficient is its use of transnational electronic networks. The presence of shared values, or at least of a pool of shared suspicions, among the protesters combines with easy communication to build and exploit globe-spanning social capital of a bonding type.

The Internet offers the ability to gather tiny minorities from vast populations, giving them an unprecedented collective weight. Some such groups would argue that they are thereby only acquiring some counterweight to the internationally pooled power long available, at much greater expense, to their opponents in business, crime, terrorism, and government. In this view, there is lots of international social capital, but it operates mainly to bond those sharing views that are sharply at odds with those of others. In this sense, the ability of advanced communications to broaden the scope of rapid organization helps to build social capital, but it is of a type that may serve the narrower interests of the group while threatening the legitimate aspirations of the unrepresented and increasing the possibilities of escalated conflict. The need is for more international social capital, especially of the bridging and linking types. Bridges are needed between those with diverging views, and they must be matched by trust and information flows linking those located at different levels in various hierarchies.

It is perhaps ironic that the summit process, which was intended to build bridging social capital among national leaders with an eye to developing domestic policies and international rules for mutual benefit, should come to be pilloried in almost the opposite light – as a tool of corporate interests working to exploit the masses for the greed of the few. The first summits were mainly personal meetings whose public markings were only news-less communiqués and some photo opportunities. They have since become large media events, thereby inviting broader attention and becoming the focal point for an extraordinarily broad range of protests. The protests have come to dominate planning for the events, to drive policy discussions from the media coverage, and to create rather than to heal cleavages among interest groups. There has been one positive result – an attempt to broaden summit agendas to include institutional issues (Ostry 2001) that, as I argued earlier, are of equal or greater importance than are conventional trade and macroeconomic issues. But this broadening is regarded by some protestors as defensive window dressing, unlikely to gain constructive collaboration by nongovernmental organizations and outsiders who share these broader views. In part, this is because some of the most vociferous and violent members of the loose coalition of protestors are frankly anarchistic in motivation and see no value in making democratic governance work, at least in anything like its current form. In the resulting vacuum, those who prefer the absence of effective international rules simply get on with their business. In the absence of a framework, power rules; and in a communications-rich world stealthy power rules most effectively.

Within this context, what is the benefit of the current summit process? And of high-profile international meetings in general? Since progress towards the goals described in the previous section will in any case be made at the working level, meetings at the highest level are of value chiefly for marking the launch or the successful completion of joint ventures. But if such messages are in any event being lost in the reporting of violent protests, then the summits may come to be an impediment to progress. Their loss would be seen by many as a loss of attention to global issues, and alternative venues would need to be found. Lower-profile meetings and peer-to-peer working groups are probably the best way for governments and non-governmental organizations alike to provide international transfers and to build the international frameworks required to enable the poorest countries to reap the best and reject the worst that globalization has to offer. If this means a slower pace for the evolution of new initiatives for trade, environment, and other issues requiring international commitments, then that may be part of the price to be paid for restoring the fortunes of international democracy.

Whither Canada?

The title of a previous section suggests a dichotomy – that there is a Canadian choice to be made between seeking ever closer bilateral relations with the United States and adopting a more multilateral strategy. Is this dichotomy a real one? Cannot Canada choose to improve and even to extend bilateral relations with the US without foreclosing chances to build a more balanced global economy and society? My general answer to this question is nuanced: there are places where a dominant bilateral focus would limit Canada's abilities to contribute to a better global system, but an appropriately defined multilateral strategy could provide due and timely attention to bilateral issues. Given the size and locations of Canada and the US, bilateral issues will often be at the top of Canadian policy agendas, whatever the nature of the overall strategy within which these issues are settled. To achieve the right balance, it is necessary to define a balanced multilateral strategy whose details reflect circumstances that alter from one bilateral application to the next.

I have previously presented evidence and arguments suggesting that further bilateral deepening of north-south economic relations, such as adopting the US dollar, offers little or no direct economic or political advantage. This, in turn, suggests that a more multilateral strategy would not jeopardize any important bilateral opportunities. In any case, as long as the multilateral strategy provides a solid basis for dealing with bilateral issues, whether relating to softwood lumber, film subsidies, health care, or water, then it need not pose any threat to constructive solutions to bilateral problems or to imaginative projects for bilateral cooperation.

What might be the main principles for a multilateral strategy? First and foremost, it should pass the fundamental test of general adoption; that is, it should work as well or better if it were adopted not just by Canada but by all countries. Second, the fallback principle suggests that the strategy should produce good results even if it were not widely shared by other countries. Since establishing common cause internationally is a slow and uneven process, one implication of the two principles is likely to be that the scope and nature of international rules and collaboration will differ markedly from one issue to another and even from one decade to the next. There may then also be international agreements that are accepted and joined, at least at first, by a minority of countries, with subsequent accession depending on the attractions of joining and the methods adopted to deal with free riders (i.e., those who want to receive the benefits from cooperation without paying their share of the costs). For example, individual tax haven countries are likely to benefit most from a system in which many or most of their competitors in this field have accepted some international framework of acceptable practices, while they themselves are able to exploit the margins lying beyond those limits.

This raises the question of linkage, an issue that has become of central importance in the WTO, the IMF, and other multilateral organizations. Should accession to the WTO be made to depend upon adequate domestic respect for human rights, health and safety, and the environment? What linkage should there be between IMF support and reforms of domestic economic and political institutions? Given what I have already argued to be very large international differences in values, priorities, and institutions, it is likely that linkage can quickly become either imperialistic (in the sense of forcing some countries' institutional preferences onto other countries) or counterproductive (in the sense of ruling out what otherwise might have been improvements to the international order). Thus it would seem appropriate, as far as possible, to limit linkage to activities central to the agreement or sphere of action under discussion and to tailor agreements so as to naturally limit the extent of the free-rider problem. This means structuring them so as to make sure that the major advantages flow to adhering countries, which, in turn, would agree to limit their own freedom of action for the greater good.

What about objectives for individual countries and for the world as a whole? Three points spring to mind, or at least they did when I first spelled them out in a lecture about Canada given at Trent University in 1972 (Helliwell 2000, 45-6):

1   To develop trade of goods, services and capital with other countries to make best use of each country's specialized resources and of world resources used communally by all countries.
2   To obtain multilateral agreements about the rules under which trade and international relations in general take place – the establishment of international law, of tax treaties, of trade agreements, and of rules governing the international financial system and international flows of commodities, whether sold or given as aid. Some of the aspects of these arrangements are undoubtedly of value beyond the narrow economic interests of Canada, but they may be justified even in support of such interests, for the small country is the one most likely to get hurt in power plays with big trading partners. The existence of agreed rules for trade does not remove the possibilities for small countries to get squeezed, but such rules do reduce the likely costs of confrontations. There is an alternative strategy for the small country – to stick by a large ally with common interests, and to rely on the power of that ally. This strategy, however, cannot easily work for the world as a whole. If world views and bargaining positions become excessively polarized, chances increase for power confrontations between "great powers."

3 Encouragement of international transfers of wealth and knowledge from the rich to the poor. Altruism aside, this clearly aids the second goal above, and the second goal is equally clearly a pre-condition of the first.

I think these objectives are as sound now as they seemed to me then, with their emphasis on sufficient openness to exploit opportunities and transfer knowledge, rules to ensure broad access on equal terms for countries large and small, and transfers from rich to poor to enable the latter to best develop their incomes and opportunities. How would implementation now be different than it would have been thirty years ago?

If I had known then the full economic and social significance of national borders, I would have recast my third point about international transfers of wealth and knowledge. It is now more apparent than it was then that the required transfers include the capacity to design and manage institutions ranging across education, health, justice, government, and business. There is much that richer countries, especially those free of the taint of power, can do to help developing countries to build their institutional capacities. This was always known, but the evidence on border effects reminds us that the job is more important and more difficult than was once thought. The gains are also larger than might previously be thought as the development of internationally compatible institutions is likely to make all parties better off. For similar reasons, transfers of wealth in the absence of institutional capacity are likely to make all parties worse off; the donors give up wealth, and the recipients may dissipate it, frequently in ways that reduce the likelihood of achieving needed reforms.

If one believed that national borders no longer mattered, and that material and social advantages would increasingly accrue to those in the larger and more powerful nations, then that might provide some reason for Canada to focus its policies in a North American context and to achieve maximum shelter for Canada under the US umbrella. It would also suggest the need for, or at least the acquiescence in, greater alignment of domestic economic and social policies with those adopted in the United States.

If, on the contrary, the future holds at least equal promise for smaller independent countries, which have the continuing capacity to develop policies that meet local needs, then policies for countries like Canada should follow a double track. On the one hand, there would remain the option and the responsibility to develop provincial and national policies that effectively and sustainably meet the aspirations of Canadians. On the other hand, within the global context, the reality of a world of hundreds of continuing national economies linked in so many ways requires a high degree of collaborative development of the rules-based system that is needed to assure the fairness and efficiency of these ties.

What does the continuing thickness of national borders have to say about the appropriate agendas for the WTO , the IMF, and the World Bank? The first and most important point is that the continuing ability of small countries to operate successfully with thick borders means that further expansions of international densities of trade in goods and services, at least among the industrial economies, cannot be expected to provide large increases in income. Second, my recent research shows that further increases in average income levels have little influence on self-assessed well-being, while both individual and community-level measures of education, health, employment, and social capital have continuing payoffs. The combination of these two results suggests that there is no need for haste in broadening the free trade agenda into areas that might impinge upon the ability of local and national governments, and of locally based voluntary organizations, to provide the education and health, and maintain the horizontal linkages, that are seen to create a secure foundation for individual and community well-being.

For the luckier of the smaller countries, which have traditionally included Canada and the Nordic countries but have every promise of growing into a larger group more fully representative of the world's population and future, the policy agenda should include a large component that contributes to system design and to the transfer to other countries of those ideas that have been found to work at home. It is one of the advantages of being small and relatively unimportant that investigation more easily precedes advice, and advice is more likely to be treated as an asset than an intrusion. The list of possibilities is long, but this is neither the time nor the place to set it out. Here it is enough, assuming I have done it, to have made the case that a global strategy for smaller countries could represent both good policy and good will.

If faced with a foreign policy choice between a globally oriented policy and one that has its primary focus on continuing efforts to harmonize policies with those in the United States, I think that the decision is obvious. Given the evidence I have reviewed, the latter policy is likely to represent bad economics and bad politics. North America is destined, through the joint forces of demography and catch-up, to be a smaller and smaller share of the world economy. To focus emphasis on the smaller part of the global pie may seem attractive during booming times in the United States economy, but would be a short-sighted strategy.

Fortunately, it is possible for Canada to maintain a balanced set of foreign polices that is in accord with the facts and opportunities of global markets, has a suitably broad view of the world and its needs, and still deals in a timely and consistent way with bilateral relations between this country and the United States. To implement the broad objectives outlined above, in a manner that reflects the patchwork reality of nation-states, demands joint attention to global system building and the specific problems and opportunities in each bilateral relation. To emphasize unduly the bilateral relation poses a double risk. The first is that it would ignore more attractive options elsewhere that are foreclosed by an asymmetric policy; the second is that a global perception that Canada has chosen to live under the US umbrella would limit Canada's ability to act as an independent advisor and broker in the design of the international system.

In some cases, the best Canadian contribution is as a partner in a group of potentially like-minded states concerned with dealing with questions of system design and aid reform. Simultaneously, the specific problems and opportunities of each bilateral border can be addressed in a manner consistent with the overall strategy. Thus attempts to smooth border-crossings on the land border with the United States should be dealt with locally, reflecting the big differences in issues that arise across the width of the two countries in a manner that dovetails with the management of Canada's air and sea linkages with other countries. The broad objectives should include easing legitimate movements while maintaining the rule of domestic and international law.

The final result of well-designed national and international policies would, I predict, include continued border effects of the sorts I have documented here. These would not represent evidence of border restrictions; rather, they would reflect the fact that, for now and the foreseeable future, geographic, social and political distance acts to make it cheaper and safer to use familiar and trusted institutions and pathways. If new and better institutions and pathways are to be built, whether within or across national borders, then it will be important to build them in ways that broaden rather than diminish the underlying bedrock of shared trust.

The foregoing paragraphs are drawn directly from my last attempt (Helliwell 2000, 46-9) to spell out a balanced multilateral strategy for international policies. How would I change the emphasis on the basis of the new well-being research reported in Chapter 2 and in the wake of the terrorist attacks of September 11, 2001?

The well-being research suggests that the importance of the social fabric is even greater than I had previously thought, so that, to the extent there is any perceived trade-off between sustaining the social fabric and increasing incomes, the former now appears to have a larger and faster-growing importance than was then thought. The September 11 attacks have been described by some in the United States, by analogy with Pearl Harbor, as the start of a third world war. For Canadians with still-vivid memories of the FLQ kidnappings and murder of 1970, and the Air India sabotage of 1985, it is more natural to treat the new terrorism as the work of clandestine cells of extremists. This form of organization makes it impossible for the perpetrators to be easily found, let alone eradicated by mass reprisals. Indeed, it is frequently the purpose of such extremists to tempt their victims, or their governments, into mass reprisals that will help to breed a new generation of terrorists willing to take the lives of innocents and to further threaten the possibility of national and international efforts to improve well-being.

Ever-faster and more widespread distribution of images has the potential for destroying as much as for building shared responses. For example, a single image of youthful Palestinians cheering news of the terrorist attacks might have posed as much risk to future peace as would have another fuel-laden plane. On one side of a potential religious and political cleavage the image was treated by some as evidence that the terrorists were simply the visible part of a widespread intent to wage war on the United States and to thus provide the incentive and need for massive military retaliation. On the other side of that looming divide, the widespread distribution of the image was treated as evidence of a US willingness and wish to demonize large parts of the Arab world. Images of damaged mosques in Canada have similar power to create distrust and to deepen cleavages.

How does this relate to the recent research results? The well-being research and social capital research both show the strong local and national basis of many linkages of social trust and understanding. Where global norms and networks are thin, and local ones are strong, there are greater risks that terrorist acts by individuals from elsewhere will be blamed on the nations or religions of their origin or affiliation. Atrocities put extreme pressures on the fragile fabric of internationally shared norms; yet it is precisely in the wake of such atrocities when shared norms, and the ability to design responses that will reduce rather than raise the risks of future atrocities, are most crucial. These events place great internal pressures on diverse societies such as Canada as these are the societies where external cleavages are more likely to have internal echoes. Yet these are also the societies that are best placed to help avoid international cleavages based on nationality, race, and religion since repeated friendly contacts in schools, jobs, and communities contribute to shared networks and norms that can help to avoid the escalation and extension of conflict so clearly desired by the terrorists.

The September 11 attacks had two more specific effects on Canada and on the agenda for Canadian policies. US desires for heightened border security led initially to long delays in clearing both people and goods moving from Canada to the United States. These delays led some to advocate the establishment of a common North American security perimeter, with the proposals extending in some cases to a customs union, common visa requirements, and even a common currency. I was inclined then, and have been more inclined since, to focus attention on risk assessments and to argue that increasing inspections of goods flows across the Canada-US border was, if anything, less likely to turn up evidence of terrorist activity than would random checks of trucks travelling along the US Interstate highway system. In either case it was not a cost-effective way of reducing the risk of further terrorist attacks. The increased attention to border issues had some positive results, however, as the addition of new resources to border clearances of goods and people entering the United States from Canada gave some prospect of removing the long-standing imbalance. Prior to September 11, there were approximately 50 percent more staff and open lanes northbound than southbound, with a correspondingly higher number of discoveries of criminal activity. If the additional resources projected to police southbound movements are rationally deployed, then they could lead to southbound movements being faster than they were before September 11, even without any further efforts to create a common North American security perimeter. Increasing the extent of shared information on security suspects, and the development of enhanced and more harmonized clearance of goods at major international ports, could also contribute to increased security, reduced crime, and less risk of terrorism in both countries. As for the international movements of potential terrorists, the biggest risks for both countries remain commercial airline flights from overseas. These risks are, of course, best addressed by increasing pre-clearance efforts in overseas points of embarkation. These improvements require collaboration with overseas governments, and the posting of Canadian clearance officers overseas (as Canada had already done, to considerable effect, well before September 11), without any special need for linking Canadian efforts with those of the United States (beyond the need for both countries to share in more effective multinational efforts).

Another consequence of September 11, especially as the so-called war on terrorism enters new phases, has been to expose new threats to the multilateral rules and institutions created in the middle of the twentieth century to govern international relations. In the aftermath of September 11 there has been increased unilateral action by the United States, supported initially by strong sympathy and support from coalition partners, NATO, and the UN. The further these actions get from bringing the atrocity's perpetrators to justice, the more gaps are exposed between the values, methods, public opinions, and powers of the members of the international community. More than ever before, the United States has the capacity, and possibly the intent, to take actions without the active support of the broader international community or even its NATO partners. This could pose ever-greater challenges for those who believe, as do most Canadians, in the international rule of law. In these circumstances, it is more important than ever, from a global perspective, that Canada continue to maintain a sufficient degree of independence from the United States in order to be able to provide a mediating voice and to influence the evolution of the global architecture.

Finally, I need to respond to a natural reaction some readers have had to what I have said thus far. My analysis of the well-being evidence has led me to argue that the Scandinavian aspects of Canadian life are more important to well-being than are further increases in GDP per capita, while the borders evidence suggests that the capacity to maintain the relevant differences in polices and attitudes is still intact. But does this take sufficiently into account that the Scandinavian countries are in some sense more insulated from foreign influences than is Canada and that they are far less reliant on a single dominant trading partner? One response to this is that the separateness of Canadian attitudes and actions has been maintained for more than a century in the face of such special circumstances and, to some extent, even because of them. Circumstances make Canadians uniquely reliant on US trade and aware of (and no doubt influenced by) US attitudes and culture. Perhaps the most important difference between the Canadian and Scandinavian prospects of maintaining policies and social institutions that reflect the values of their citizens relate to flows of information and, hence, to beliefs about even the possibilities for independent action. As I have noted elsewhere (Helliwell 2001a), the predominance of northbound over southbound information flows between the United States and Canada means that Canadians are much more informed about the US than vice versa, and the predominance of US information and images may lead Canadians to underestimate the extent to which they are different, and to be unaware of the extent to which their own views may be shared by their fellow citizens. And these attitudes themselves are subject to change in response to changes in migration, education, and all forms of culture. Of course, the size, power, global reach, and relative insularity of the United States means that such asymmetries are not unique to Canada but, rather, are felt in all countries. Canada's closeness in distance and language coupled with the appearance of all the US networks on most Canadian television screens combine to make the Canadian case a special one.

Perhaps it is therefore inevitable, and even rational, for Canadians to think self-consciously about their values and circumstances at least once in each generation. Only thus can they ensure the election of governments that reflect their values and, thereby, ensure that Canada does not unwittingly drift in directions that threaten its future well-being.

Notes

1   The "nominal exchange rate" is the price of one currency in terms of another – just what is reported in the newspaper or at the airport foreign exchange kiosk. The "real exchange rate" is the nominal exchange rate adjusted for changes in price levels. If e is the domestic currency price of foreign exchange, P the domestic price level, and P^* the foreign price level, then the real exchange rate is eP^*/P. If either the exchange rate or prices move so as to maintain purchasing power parity, then the real exchange rate will always be 1.0.

2   The forward exchange differential is the difference between the forward and spot exchange rates, often measured as a proportion of the current spot rate and sometimes restated in annual terms. If the current price of foreign exchange (known as the spot rate) is S, and the forward rate for delivery in one year is F, then the forward exchange differential, in proportionate terms, is $(F\text{-}S)/S$.

3   See Dekle (1996) for Japan; Sinn (1992) for the US; and Bayoumi and Rose (1993) for the UK.

4   When legal systems are different, as they are more likely to be between countries than within regions of a country, then trade is likely to be especially dependent upon mutual trust and to be threatened when that trust is absent. Hence Anderson and Marcouiller (1999) show that international trade is severely reduced where corruption is high. They argue that this is much of the reason why trade intensities are much higher among the OECD countries than among countries in general.

5   For example, the 1999 Annual Report of the European Bank for Reconstruction and Development estimated that, of the twenty-five former East Bloc countries monitored by the EBRD, only Poland and Slovenia had regained their 1989 levels of real GDP by 1998, while the 1998 levels of real GDP in Russia and Ukraine were only 55 percent and 37 percent, respectively, of what they had been in 1989.

6   If it is assumed that greater product variety is the source of increased welfare for consumers, as is done in several trade theories (especially the recent work of Anderson and van Wincoop [2001]), then further increases in trade intensity can show increases in welfare even if there are no cost advantages. However, psychological experiments (e.g., Iyengar and Lepper 1999) show that increases in product variety, after some fairly

limited amount, can reduce consumer satisfaction by increasing their difficulties in making decisions among too many alternatives and increasing the likelihood of subsequent regret following their eventual decisions.

7   Gould (1994) provides a comparable study of the trade effects of American immigration.

8   For a more detailed view of how I saw these issues at that time, see Helliwell (2000, 2001a).

9   Many others have also seen the advantages of studying social capital and education within the broader context of well-being. The title of the OECD (2001) report on the effects of human and social capital is *The Well-Being of Nations*. In addition, many of the attempts to enrich the range and significance of the national accounts as measures of economic welfare (e.g., Offer 2000; Osberg and Sharpe 2001) have a similar motivation, as do, of course, the United Nations Development Program (UNDP) assessments discussed in the text.

10 See Argyle (1986); Argyle and Martin (1991); and Myers and Diener (1995) for earlier contributions. See Diener et al. (1999) for a comprehensive survey; Myers (2000) for a recent assessment; and Diener (2000) for a proposal to publish a national index of subjective well-being.

11 The Almeda county study of Berkman and Syme (1979) remains the classic reference.

12 There are two reasons for using the answers to this question rather than to questions dealing more explicitly with happiness or unhappiness. One is that the measure of life satisfaction occurs on a more extended scale, which provides more explanatory power for the equation. The other is that psychological studies have shown that answers to questions about life satisfaction tend to reflect a longer-term and more stable assessment than do those asking about happiness, as was predicted many centuries ago by Aristotle.

13 This is a slightly modified form of two-way fixed effects estimation. It is necessary to use regional groupings of countries rather than separate constant terms for each country because the array has many fewer than $3n$ country observations, where n is the total number of countries and 3 is the number of survey waves. This is because the number of included countries is on an increasing trend, and some of the original, mainly OECD, countries are not in both of the succeeding waves. The country groups included are the former USSR, Eastern Europe, Latin America, Asia (including Japan and India), other developing countries, and Scandinavia. The residual base group includes all of the other OECD countries in the survey.

14 "In general, do you think that people can be trusted, or, alternatively, that you can't be too careful when dealing with people?" This is coded 1.0 if the person chooses the high-trust alternative.

15 Other studies of the effects of income on well-being include Easterlin (1974, 1995); Oswald (1997); Smith and Razzell (1975); Brickman, Coates, and Janoff-Bulman (1978); Gardner and Oswald (2001); and Frey and Stutzer (2000, 2002).

16 For a survey of much of the earlier work, see Côté (1994).

17 See, for example, Courchene and Harris (1999); Laidler (1999); Murray (1999); McCallum (2000); and the papers in Bank of Canada (2001).

References

Alesina, Alberto, Rafael Di Tella, and Robert MacCulloch. 2001. "Inequality and Happiness: Are Europeans and Americans Different?" NBER Working Paper No. 8198, Cambridge, National Bureau of Economic Research.

Almond, Gabriel A., and Sidney Verba. 1963. *The Civic Culture: Political Attitudes and Democracy in Five Nations*. Princeton: Princeton University Press.

Anderson, James E., and Douglas Marcouiller. 1999. "Trade, Insecurity and Home Bias: An Empirical Investigation." NBER Working Paper No. 7000, Cambridge, National Bureau of Economic Research.

Anderson, James E., and Eric van Wincoop. 2001. "Gravity with Gravitas: A Solution to the Border Puzzle." NBER Working Paper No. 8079, Cambridge, National Bureau of Economic Research.

Argyle, Michael. 1986. *The Psychology of Happiness*. London: Methuen.

Argyle, Michael, and Maryanne Martin. 1991. "The Psychological Causes of Happiness." In Fritz Strack, Michael Argyle, and Norbert Schwartz, eds., *Subjective Well-Being: An Interdisciplinary Perspective*, 77-100. Oxford: Pergamon Press.

Backus, David, Patrick Kehoe, and Finn Kydland. 1992. "International Real Business Cycles." *Journal of Political Economy* 100 (August): 745-75.

Bank of Canada. 2001. *Revisiting the Case for Flexible Exchange Rates*. Conference proceedings, November 2000. Ottawa: Bank of Canada.

Baxter, Marianne, and Urban J. Jermann. 1997. "The International Diversification Puzzle Is Worse Than You Think." *American Economic Review* 87 (1): 170-80.

Bayoumi, Tamim, and Andrew Rose. 1993. "Domestic Saving and Intra-National Capital Flows." *European Economic Review* 37 (6): 1197-202.

Berkman, L.F., and S.L. Syme. 1979. "Social Networks, Host Resistance, and Mortality: A Nine-Year Follow-Up Study of Almeda County

Residents." *American Journal of Epidemiology* 109: 186-204.

Blank, Rebecca M., and Maria J. Hanratty. 1993. "Responding to Need: A Comparison of Social Safety Nets in Canada and the United States." In David Card and Richard B. Freeman, eds., *Small Differences That Matter: Labor Markets and Income Maintenance in Canada and the United States*, 191-231. Chicago: University of Chicago Press.

Brickman, Philip, Dan Coates, and Ronnie Janoff-Bulman. 1978. "Lottery Winners and Accident Victims: Is Happiness Relative?" *Journal of Personality and Social Psychology* 36 (8): 917-27.

Burtless, Gary, Robert Z. Lawrence, Robert E. Litan, and Robert J. Shapiro. 1998. *Globaphobia: Confronting Fears about Open Trade.* Washington: Brookings Institution.

Chen, Natalie. 2001. "Intra-National Versus International Trade in the European Union: Why Do National Borders Matter?" Brussels: Université Libre de Bruxelles.

Clark, A.E., and A.J. Oswald. 1994. "Unhappiness and Unemployment." *Economic Journal* 104: 648-59.

Coe, D.T., and E. Helpman. 1995. "International R&D Spillovers." *European Economic Review* 39 (5): 859-87.

Côté, Agathe. 1994. "Exchange Rate Volatility and Trade: A Survey." Bank of Canada Working Paper Nos. 94-5, Ottawa.

Courchene, Thomas J., and Richard G. Harris. 1999. "From Fixing to Monetary Union: Options for North American Currency Integration." C.D. Howe Institute Commentary 127, Toronto.

Davis, Donald R., et al. 1997. "Using International and Japanese Regional Data to Determine When the Factor Abundance Theory of Trade Works." *American Economic Review* 87 (3): 421-46.

Dekle, Robert. 1996. "Savings-Investment Associations and Capital Mobility: On the Evidence from Japanese Regional Data." *Journal of International Economics* 41 (1-2): 53-72.

Diener, Ed. 2000. "Subjective Well-Being: The Science of Happiness and a Proposal for a National Index." *American Psychologist* 55 (1): 34-43.

Diener, E., E.M. Suh, R.E. Lucas, and H.L Smith. 1999. "Subjective Well-Being: Three Decades of Progress." *Psychological Bulletin* 125 (2): 276-302.

Di Tella, R., R.J. MacCulloch, and A.J. Oswald. 2001. "Preferences over Inflation and Unemployment: Evidence from Surveys of Happiness." *American Economic Review* 91 (1): 335-41.

Easterlin, R.A. 1974. "Does Economic Growth Improve the Human Lot? Some Empirical Evidence." In P.A. David and M.W. Reder, eds., *Nations and Households in Economic Growth*, 89-125. New York: Academic Press.

—. 1995. "Will Raising the Incomes of All Increase the Happiness of All?" *Journal of Economic Behaviour and Organization* 27 (1): 35-48.

Emes, Joel, and Tony Hahn. 2001. "Measuring Development: An Index of Human Progress." Fraser Institute Occasional Paper 36, Vancouver.

Engel, Charles, and J.H. Rogers. 1996. "How Wide Is the Border?" *American Economic Review* 86 (December): 1112-25.

Feldstein, Martin S., and Charles Horioka. 1980. "Domestic Savings and International Capital Flows." *Economic Journal* 90 (June): 314-29.

Finnie, Ross. 2001. "The Brain Drain: Myth and Reality – What It Is and What Should Be Done." IRPP Policy Paper. Montreal: Institute for Research on Public Policy.

Fischer, Stanley. 2001. "Distinguished Lecture on Economics in Government – Exchange Rate Regimes: Is the Bipolar View Correct?" *Journal of Economic Perspectives* 15 (2): 3-24.

Fortin, Pierre. 1999. *The Canadian Standard of Living: Is There a Way Up?* Toronto: C.D. Howe Institute Benefactors Lecture.

—. 2001. "Interest Rates, Unemployment and Inflation." In Keith Banting, Andrew Sharpe, and France St-Hilaire, eds., *The Review of Economic Performance and Social Progress*, 113-30. Montreal and Ottawa: Institute for Research on Public Policy and Centre for the Study of Living Standards.

Frank, Jeff, and Éric Bélair. 1999. *South of the Border: An Analysis of Results from the Survey of 1995 Graduates Who Moved to the United States.* Ottawa: Human Development Canada and Statistics Canada.

Frankel, Jeffrey, and Andrew Rose. 2000. "Estimating the Effect of Currency Unions on Trade and Output." NBER Working Paper No. 7857, Cambridge, National Bureau of Economic Research.

French, Kenneth R., and James M. Poterba. 1991. "Investor Diversification and International Equity Markets." *American Economic Review* 81 (2): 222-6.

Frey, Bruno S., and Alois Stutzer. 2000. "Happiness, Economy and Institutions." *Economic Journal* 110 (466): 918-38.

—. 2002. *Happiness and Economics.* Princeton: Princeton University Press.

Gardner, Jonathan, and Andrew Oswald. 2001. "Does Money Buy Happiness? A Longitudinal Study Using Data on Windfalls." University of Warwick Working Paper. Coventry: University of Warwick.

Gaudry, Marc, U. Blum, and John McCallum. 1996. "A First Gross Measure of Unexploited Market Potential." In S. Urban, ed., *Europe's Challenges.* Weisbaden: Gabler.

Gottschalk, Peter, and Timothy M. Smeeding. 1997. "Cross-National Comparisons of Earnings and Income Inequality." *Journal of Economic Literature* 35 (June): 633-87.

Gould, David M. 1994. "Immigrant Links to the Home Country: Implications for U.S. Bilateral Trade Flows." *Review of Economics and Statistics* 76 (2): 302-16.

Greif, Avner. 1992. "Institutions and International Trade: Lessons From the Commercial Revolution." *American Economic Review* 82 (2): 128-33.

Grossman, Gene M. 1997. "Comment." In J.A. Frankel, ed., *The Regionalization of the World Economy*, 29-31. Chicago: University of Chicago Press.

Hart, Oliver. 1995. *Firms, Contracts, and Financial Structure*. Oxford: Clarendon Press.

Hazeldine, Tim. 2000. "Review of *How Much Do National Borders Matter?*" *Canadian Journal of Economics* 33 (1): 288-92.

Head, Keith, and John Ries. 1998. "Immigration and Trade Creation: Evidence from Canada." *Canadian Journal of Economics* 31 (1): 47-62.

Head, Keith, and Thierry Mayer. 2000. "Non-Europe: The Magnitude and Causes of Market Fragmentation in the EU." *Weltwirtschaftliches Archiv* 136 (2): 284-314.

Helliwell, John F. 1989. "From Now till Then: Globalization and Economic Cooperation." *Canadian Public Policy* 15 (special issue, February): S 71-7.

—. 1996a. "Convergence and Migration among Provinces." *Canadian Journal of Economics* 29 (special issue): S324-30.

—. 1996b. "Do National Borders Matter for Quebec's Trade?" *Canadian Journal of Economics* 29: 507-22.

—. 1997. "National Borders, Trade and Migration." *Pacific Economic Review* 2: 165-85.

—. 1998. *How Much Do National Borders Matter?* Washington, DC: Brookings Institution Press.

—. 1999. "Checking the Brain Drain: Evidence and Implications." *Policy Options* 20 (7) (September).

—. 2000. *Globalization: Myths, Facts and Consequences*. Toronto: C.D. Howe Institute. Benefactors Lecture 2000. Available at <www.cdhowe.org>.

—. 2001a. "Canada: Life beyond the Looking Glass." *Journal of Economic Perspectives* 15 (1): 107-24.

—. 2001b. "Social Capital, the Economy and Well-Being." In Keith Banting, Andrew Sharpe, and France St-Hilaire, eds., *The Review of Economic Performance and Social Progress*, 43-60. Montreal and Ottawa: Institute for Research on Public Policy and Centre for the Study of Living Standards. Available at <www.csls.ca>.

—. 2002a. "Measuring the Width of National Borders." *Review of International Economics* 10 (3): 517-24.

—. 2002b. "How's Life: Combining Individual and National Variables to Explain Subjective Well-Being." NBER Working Paper No. W9065, Cambridge, National Bureau of Economic Research (forthcoming in *Economic Modelling*).

—. 2002c. "Border Effects: Assessing Their Implications for Canadian Policy in a North-American Context." Prepared for an HRDC/Industry Canada conference on North American Linkages, November 2002.

Helliwell, John F., and David F. Helliwell. 2000. "Tracking UBC Graduates: Trends and Explanations." ISUMA: *Canadian Journal of Policy Research* 1 (1): 101-10. Available at <www.isuma.net>.

—. 2001. "Where Are They Now? Migration Patterns for Graduates of the University of British Columbia." In Patrick Grady and Andrew Sharpe, eds., *The State of Canadian Economics: Essays in Honour of David Slater*, 291-322. Montreal: McGill-Queen's University Press. Available at <www.csls.ca>.

Helliwell, John F., Frank C. Lee, and Hans Messinger. 1999. "Effects of the Canada-United States Free Trade Agreement on Interprovincial Trade." Industry Canada Perspectives on North American Free Trade, Series 5, Ottawa.

Helliwell, John F., and John McCallum. 1995. "National Borders Still Matter for Trade." *Policy Options/Options Politiques* 16: 44-8.

Helliwell, John F., and Ross McKitrick. 1999. "Comparing Capital Mobility Across Provincial and National Borders." *Canadian Journal of Economics* 32 (5): 1164-73.

Helliwell, John F., and Robert D. Putnam. 1995. "Economic Growth

and Social Capital in Italy." *Eastern Economic Journal* 21 (3): 295-307.

—. 1999. "Education and Social Capital." NBER Working Paper No. W7121, Cambridge, National Bureau of Economic Research.

Helliwell, John F., and Geneviève Verdier. 2001. "Measuring International Trade Distances: A New Method Applied to Estimate Provincial Border Effects in Canada." *Canadian Journal of Economics* 34 (5): 1024-41.

Hillberry, Russell. 1998. "Regional Trade and the Medicine Line: The National Border Effect in U.S. Commodity Flow Data." *Journal of Borderland Studies* 8 (2): 1-17.

—. 1999. "Explaining the Border Effect: What Can We Learn from Disaggregated Commodity Flow Data?" Mimeo, Washington, DC.

Inglehart, Ronald, et al. 2000. "World Values Surveys and European Values Surveys, 1981-1984, 1990-1993, and 1995-1997." Computer File, ICPSR Version. Ann Arbor, Michigan: Inter-university Consortium for Political and Social Research.

Iqbal, Mahmood. 1999. *Are We Losing Our Minds? Trends, Determinants and the Role of Taxation in Brain Drain to the United States*. Ottawa: Conference Board of Canada.

Iyengar S.S., and M.R. Lepper. 1999. "Rethinking the Value of Choice: A Cultural Perspective on Intrinsic Motivation." *Journal of Personality and Social Psychology* 76: 349-66.

Kapur, Devesh. 2001. "Diasporas and

Technology Transfer." *Journal of Human Development* 2 (2): 265-86.

Kaufmann, Daniel, Aart Kraay, and Pablo Zoido-Lobatoni. 1999a. "Aggregating Governance Indicators." World Bank Policy Research Department Working Paper No. 2195.

—. 1999b. "Governance Matters." World Bank Policy Research Department Working Paper No. 2196.

Keller, Wolfgang. 2002. "Geographic Localization of International Technology Diffusion." *American Economic Review* 92 (1): 120-42.

Laidler, David. 1999. "What Do the Fixers Want to Fix? The Debate about Canada's Exchange Rate Regime." Toronto: C.D. Howe Institute (Commentary 131).

Lemieux, Thomas. 1993. "Unions and Wage Inequality in Canada and the United States." In David Card and Richard B. Freeman, eds., *Small Differences That Matter: Labor Markets and Income Maintenance in Canada and the United States*, 69-108. Chicago: University of Chicago Press.

McCallum, John. 1995. "National Borders Matter: Canada-U.S. Regional Trade Patterns." *American Economic Review* 85: 615-23.

—. 2000. *Engaging the Debate: Costs and Benefits of a North American Common Currency*. Toronto: Royal Bank of Canada Current Analysis. Available at <www.royalbank.com/economics>.

Mackay, J. Ross. 1958. "The Interactance Hypothesis and Boundaries in Canada: A Preliminary Study." *Canadian Geographer* 11: 1-8.

Marer, Paul, and Salvatore Zecchini, eds. 1991. *The Transition to a Market Economy*. Vol. 1: *The Broad Issues*. Paris: OECD.

Murray, John. 1999. "Why Canada Needs a Flexible Exchange Rate." Bank of Canada Working Paper No. 99-12, Ottawa.

Myers, David G. 2000. "The Funds, Friends and Faith of Happy People." *American Psychologist* 55 (1): 56-67.

Myers, David G., and Ed Diener. 1995. "Who is Happy?" *Psychological Science* 6 (1): 10-19.

Nie, Norman H., Jane Junn, and Kenneth Stehlik-Barry. 1996. *Education and Democratic Citizenship in America*. Chicago: University of Chicago Press.

Nitsch, Volker. 2000a. "National Borders and International Trade: Evidence from the European Union." *Canadian Journal of Economics* 33 (4): 1091-105.

—. 2000b. *It's Not Right but It's Okay: On the Measurement of Intra- and International Trade Distances*. Berlin: Bank Gesselschaft.

—. 2001. *Statistics Canada 2, Statistisches Bundesamt 1. What Does German Data Tell Us about the Home Bias in International Trade?* Berlin: Bank Gesselschaft.

Offer, Avner. 2000. *Economic Welfare Measurements and Human Well-Being*. Oxford: University of Oxford Press (Discussion Papers in Economic and Social History 34).

Organization for Economic Co-operation and Development. 2001. *The Well-Being of Nations: The Role of Human and Social Capital*. Paris: OECD Centre for Educational Research and Innovation.

Osberg, Lars G., and Andrew Sharpe. 2001. "Comparisons of Trends in GDP and Economic Well-Being." In John F. Helliwell, ed., *The Contribution of Human and Social Capital to Sustained Economic Growth and Well-Being*, 310-51. Ottawa: HDRC and OECD. Available at <www.hrdc-drhc.gc.ca/arb>.

Ostry, Sylvia. 2001. "Dissent.Com: How the NGOs Are Re-making the WTO." *Policy Options* (June): 6-15.

Oswald, A.J. 1997. "Happiness and Economic Performance." *Economic Journal* 107 (445): 1815-31.

Parsley, David C., and Shang-Jin Wei. 2000. "Border, Border, Wide and Far, How We Wonder What You Are." Paper presented at the Gerzensee Conference on "Lessons from Intranational Economics for International Economics."

Persson, Torsten, and Guido Tabellini. 1994. "Is Inequality Harmful for Growth?" *American Economic Review* 84 (3): 600-21.

Putnam, Robert D. 1993. *Making Democracy Work: Civic Traditions in Modern Italy*. Princeton: Princeton University Press.

—. 1995. "Tuning In, Tuning Out: The Strange Disappearance of Social Capital in America." *PS: Political Science and Politics* 28: 664-83.

—. 2000. *Bowling Alone: The Collapse and Revival of American Community*. New York: Simon and Schuster.

—. 2001. "Social Capital: Measurement and Consequences." In John F. Helliwell, ed., *The Contribution of Human and Social Capital to Sustained Economic Growth and Well-Being*, 117-35. Ottawa: HDRC and OECD. Available at <www.hrdc-drhc.gc.ca/arb>. See also the summary version in ISUMA 2 (1): 41-52, available at <www.isuma.net>.

Raiser, Martin. 1997. "Informal Institutions, Social Capital and Economic Transition: Reflections on a Neglected Dimension." European Bank for Reconstruction and Development Working Paper No. 25, London.

Rice, Tom W., and Jan L. Feldman. 1997. "Civic Culture and Democracy from Europe to America." *Journal of Politics* 59 (4): 1143-72.

Rose, Andrew. 2000. "One Money, One Market: Estimating the Effects of Common Currencies on Trade." *Economic Policy* 30: 7-46.

Rose, Andrew K., and Eric van Wincoop. 2001. "National Money as a Barrier to International Trade: The Real Case for Currency Union." *American Economic Review Papers and Proceedings* 91 (2): 386-90.

Ross, Nancy A., Michael C. Wolfson, James R. Dunn, Jean-Marie Berthelot, George A. Kaplan, and John W. Lynch. 1999. "Relation

Between Income Inequality and Mortality in Canada and the United States: Cross-sectional Assessment Using Census Data and Vital Statistics." *British Medical Journal* 320: 898-902.

Sachs, Jeffrey D., and Andrew Warner. 1995. "Economic Reform and the Process of Global Integration." *Brookings Papers on Economic Activity* 1: 1-118.

Sinn, Stefan. 1992. "Saving-Investment Correlations and Capital Mobility: On the Evidence from Annual Data." *Economic Journal* 102: 1162-70.

Smith, S., and P. Razzell. 1975. *The Pools Winners*. London: Caliban Books.

Thom, Rodney, and Brendan Walsh. 2001. "The Effect of a Common Currency on Trade: The Ending of Ireland's Sterling Link as a Case Study." Cambridge: National Bureau of Economic Research. Draft paper for the international seminar on macroeconomics, Dublin, June 2001.

Trefler, Daniel. 1999. "The Long and the Short of the Canada-U.S. Free Trade Agreement." Industry Canada Perspectives on North American Free Trade, Series 6, Ottawa.

Wagner, Don. 2000. "Taxes Do Matter for the Brain Drain." Paper prepared for the Annual Meetings of the Canadian Economics Association, Vancouver, June.

Wei, Shang-Jin. 1996. "Intra-National versus International Trade: How Stubborn Are Nations in Global Integration?" NBER Working Paper No. 5531, Cambridge, National Bureau of Economic Research.

Wolf, Holger. 2000. "Intranational Home Bias in Trade." *Review of Economics and Statistics* 82 (4): 555-63.

Wolfe, Barbara, and Robert Haveman. 2001. "Accounting for the Social and Non-Market Effects of Education." In John F. Helliwell, ed., *The Contribution of Human and Social Capital to Sustained Economic Growth and Well-Being*, 221-50. Ottawa: HDRC and OECD. Available at <www.hrdc-drhc.gc.ca/arb>.

Wolfson, M., G. Kaplan, J. Lynch, N. Ross, and E. Backlund. 1999. "The Relationship between Inequality and Mortality Is Not a Statistical Artefact: An Empirical Demonstration." *British Medical Journal* 319: 953-7.

Wolfson, M., and B. Murphy. 2000. "Income Inequality in North America: Does the 49th Parallel Still Matter?" *Canadian Economic Observer* (August): 3.1-3.24.

Worms, Jean-Pierre. 2002. "Old and New Civic and Social Ties in France." In Robert D. Putnam, ed., *Democracies in Flux*, 137-88. New York: Oxford University Press.

Zhao, John, Doug Drew, and T. Scott Murray. 2000. "Brain Drain and Brain Gain: The Migration of Knowledge Workers from and to Canada." *Education Quarterly Review* 6 (3): 8-35.

Index

age, and well-being, 49

Bank of Canada, 67
bilateral merchandise trade, 19-20
bilateral trade data, 62
border effect, 21-3, 24, 25, 27, 28-31, 43, 54, 63, 84, 85, 87, 91; and loss of network density, 31, 32, 34, 37, 40, 74; and migration, 35-6, 37; and rich and poor countries, 33-4, 84; and trade intensity, 11, 17-18, 21, 32
brain drain. *See* migration: Canada-USA
Bretton Woods system, 62

Canada-United States Free Trade Agreement (FTA), 18, 19, 21, 28, 71, 72-3
capital, business and labour, 17
capital markets, 25-8, 67
church attendance, and well-being, 49
consumer price index, 23
consumer welfare and product variety, 34, 93n6
currency blocs, 72
currency crises, Asian, 72

de-globalizing, 17
Deutsche Mark. *See* mark, German
distance effect, 11, 17, 20, 21-2, 31, 32, 34, 35, 37, 40, 74
dollar: Canadian, 60, 66; Canadian adoption of US dollar, 66-73, 81; US, 64, 67

east-west trade. *See* trade, interprovincial (within Canada)
education, 12, 35, 43, 76, 84, 91; and social capital, 44-5, 51-2; and well-being, 49, 51-2, 54-5, 85, 94n9
Engel, Charles, 17, 21-3, 24
Euro, 59-60, 61, 62, 63, 64, 65, 66, 67, 68, 72;

and Denmark, 62, 63, 65, 66; and France, 63, 65; and Germany, 66, 68; and Italy, 65; and the Netherlands, 63, 66; and Sweden, 62, 63; and the UK, 62, 63, 65, 73
European Central Bank (ECB), 68
European Commission, 59-60, 68
European Monetary System, 62
European Parliament, 68
European Union (EU), 29-30, 60, 61, 62, 64, 65, 67, 71; and Germany, 65
exchange rate, 23-4, 25-6, 43, 59, 64, 65, 66, 71, 74, 93n1, 93n2; fixed, 62, 63, 64, 72; flexible, 23, 62, 67, 70, 72; pre-Euro, 65, 68
externalities, 44-6, 50-2, 53, 54

Feldstein, Martin S., 26, 27-8
foreign aid, 74, 75, 76-7, 83, 84, 87; in Cold War period, 76-7
formal institutions. *See* national institutions
free riders, 82, 83
free trade, 15, 85
Free Trade Agreement. *See* Canada-United States Free Trade Agreement
Fraser Institute, 47-8
FSU (former Soviet Union). *See* USSR, former

globalization, definitions of, 15-17, 77-80
globaphiles and globaphobes. *See* globalization, definitions of
gravity model, 11, 20, 29, 37, 71

health care, 43, 45, 55, 82
Heckscher-Ohlin model. *See* international trade models
Horioka, Charles, 26, 27-8

sovereignty, national: and Canada, 69; and
    European countries, 66, 68, 69; and
    Germany, 66, 68, 69; and USA, 16, 69
Soviet Union, former. *See* USSR, former
Statistics Canada, 19-20, 27
summit process, 79-81

tax, 15, 43, 54, 61, 82, 83; cheating on, 49,
    50, 51
terms-of-trade shocks, 67, 70
terrorism, 79; Air India, 87-8; and border
    security, 89-90; FLQ, 87; responses to,
    88-90; September 11, 2001 (attack on
    World Trade Towers), 87-8, 89, 90
Thom, Rodney, 63-4
trade density. *See* trade intensity
trade dependency (Canada on USA), 71-2,
    91
trade intensity, 93n6; and border effect,
    10, 11, 17-18, 21, 32; in Canada, 30;
    domestic and international, 20; rich and
    poor countries, 33-4; and social capital,
    37; and trust, 93n4
trade, interprovincial (within Canada), 10,
    17-18, 20, 22, 27, 29, 30, 60
trade, province-state (Canada-USA), 10, 17-
    18, 19-20, 22, 81
transnational corporations.
    See multinational corporations

transportation costs, 11, 16, 21, 74
trust, 35, 39, 74-5, 76, 79, 87, 88, 93n4; and
    country of origin, 39; and distance, 31,
    32, 34; and education, 44; and France,
    39; in government, 55; and
    Scandinavia, 39; standard trust
    question, 49, 94n14; and well-being,
    12, 49, 51, 52, 75

UN (United Nations), the, 90
unemployment, 47, 49
United Nations Development Program
    (UNDP), 47-8, 94n9
US-Canada Auto Pact, 71
US Federal Reserve, 67, 69, 71
USSR, former, 11-12, 31-2, 33, 39, 48, 54,
    93n5, 94n13; compared with China,
    12, 33; Mafia (Russian), 12, 32

Walsh, Brendan, 63-4
Warner, Andrew, 33
well-being, study of, 46-8, 94n9, 94n10,
    94n11, 94n12
World Bank, 85
World Trade Organization (WTO), 16,
    82, 85
World Values Survey (WVS), 39, 46, 48

Zoido-Lobatoni, Pablo, 40, 52